IF YOU CAN KILL IT
I CAN COOK IT
(...without salt)

by
SWAMP DOGG
(PhD., DDT., VD., B.S., R.F.D.)

a.k.a.
JERRY WILLIAMS JR.

I dedicate this book to my dedicated, supportive and loving wife, Yvonne, and my daughters, Desiree Anita, Antoinette Denise, Jocelyn Marie, Michelle Cecelia, and Jeri Yvonne.

VIII. GOSPEL BIRD & FAMILY

IX. PORK

X. POTATOES & YAMS

XI. VEGETABLES

XII. DESSERTS

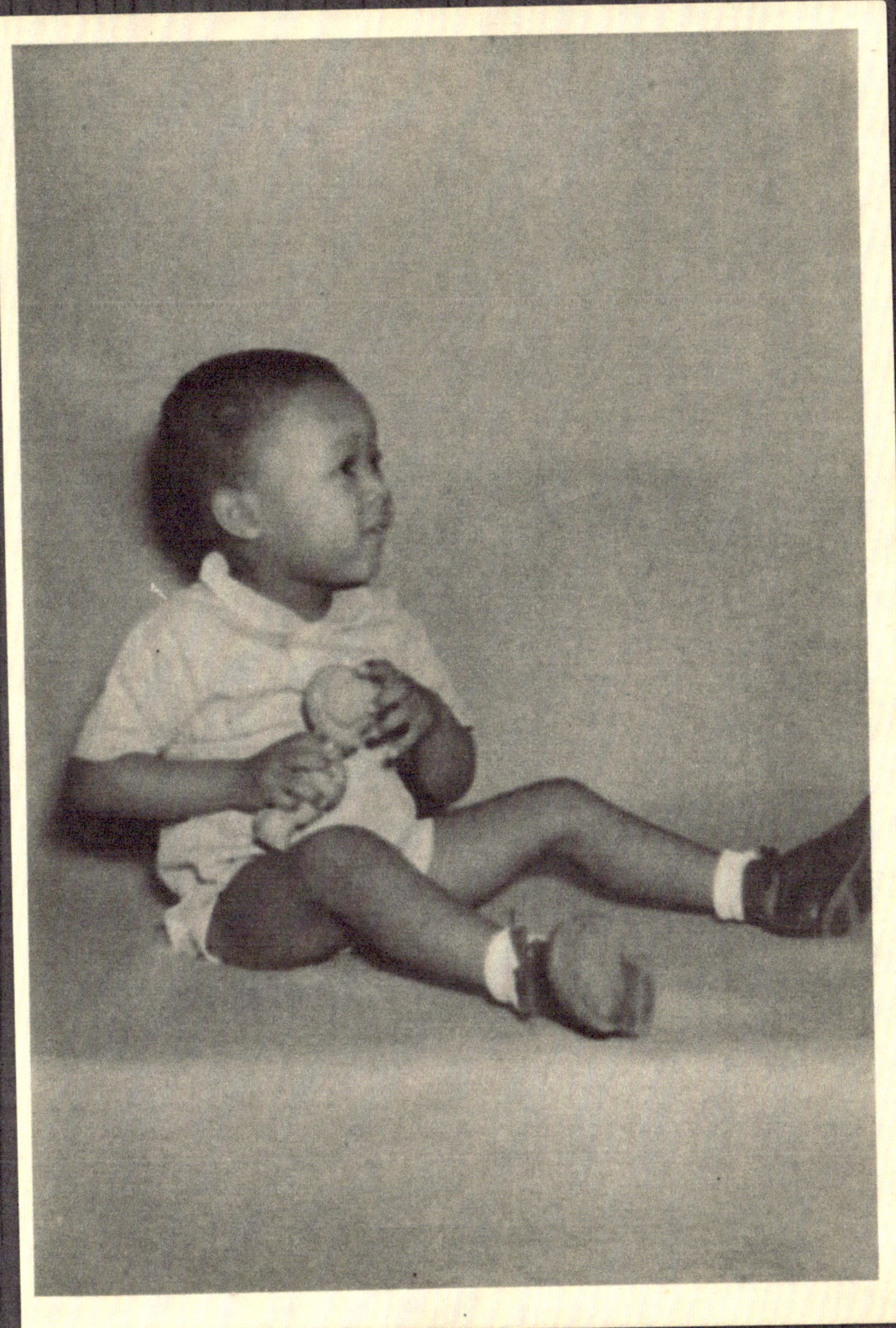

Looking... waiting... anticipating
the arrival of the love of my life,

Yvonne!!

Marriage Licenses

Applications for marriage licenses were filed by the following persons in Portsmouth during the past week:

CITY OFFICE

Jerry Williams, 23, of the U. S S. Enterprise, and Miss Vera Lee Holley, 18, of 1428 Effingham St. The marriage date was set for April 16.

Charles H. Smith, 30, of 1130 County St., and Miss Margaret D. Smith, 22, of 1215 Green St. April 15 was the proposed date of marriage.

George Pugh, 39, of 522 Riley St., Norfolk, and Miss Hattie Virginia

INTRODUCTION

It was back in 1972 when I first announced to my family and friends that I was going to write the Greatest Cook Book Ever. I told them that when it was done, Julia Childs, Amy Vanderbilt, Graham Kerr, Betty Crocker, James Beard, Craig Claiborne, Colonel Sanders, and Fannie Farmer, just to name a few, would all fade in the minds of culinary persons throughout the world. Swamp Dogg would become the new champion of the kitchen. Heralded not only by the creditable but the sleazy as well.

All this was easier said than done.

The name of my book, I told anyone who'd listen, would be... no that's been done... maybe... good, but... *The Profound Way to Cookbook*... uh uh... *The Profane Way to Cookbook*... Bullshit, I need something great like the *Encyclopedia of Cooking* or the *Joy of Cooking* or *Pearl's Kitchen* or *The World's One Hundred Best Recipes*... only... someone beat me to those (keep on thinking)...

In 1980, I still didn't have a title. But I decided the book must have a theme... French cooking (who are you kidding?)... Italian! (your sense of humor knows no bounds)... Chinese! (please, spare me)... Korean (you've mastered one dish and that's still too greasy)... German (no!) British (no!) Spanish (hell no!)... Do your own thing Swamp Dogg style (Yes! Yes! Yes!).

What dishes would be included? My favorites? My most excellent? The ones my friends salivate over? Or... all of the above? The latter is the key.

Wait!! A title is coming, *The Musical Cookbook*... Great!!... now explain it, tie it in and make it work. Well, back to the drawing board.

Several more months (years?) went by and I'm still cooking, discarding dishes, creating dishes and dissipating flour and sugar on a scale comparable only to General Mills and C&H. But as fate would have it, I did it!! My culinary genius came to the fore and I completed this masterpiece.

After that, it sat around for a while. But then my friends made a movie about me, called *Swamp Dogg Gets His Pool Painted*, and these people at Pioneer Works said they'd put out my cookbook.

And now it's here. With this book as your aid you can impress, dazzle, spellbind, fascinate, and mesmerize your friends and family.

I'm strongly recommending a $399.95 price to my publisher... and that's for paperback. Whatever they sell it for, I know it will rank with the Magna Carta, *From Here to Eternity*, the Koran, *Encyclopedia Britannica* and possibly *Devil in a Blue Dress*!

This is the book that Hemingway wanted to write, Agatha Christie couldn't, Irving Wallace needed help with, and Alex Haley didn't have enough "soul" for... I did it infallibly. Not only does it make for good cooking but good reading, 'riting and 'rithmetic (sorry, I got carried away).

Well, get to cooking!!

-S.D.

SPECIAL THANKS DEPT

To those of you who rose and wanted to rise to the occasion above and beyond the call of duty... throwing stomachs on the line and being congenial guinea pigs for my untried culinary efforts. I love all of you.

Bob Merlis, Jimmy Faines, Art Fein, Norm Goodman, Art Freeman, Rick Hocutt, Ernie Leaner, Wally Roker, Tony Leaner, Amanda Jones, Delta Ashby, Bill Liebowitz, Sam Sutherland, K.C., E. Rodney Jones, Simon Lait, Steve Price, Steve Turner, the Zimmerman twins, Larry Flint, Dale Evans, Paul Newman, Groucho Marx, Bob Newhart, Warren Lanier, Lester Maddox, F. Lee Bailey, Phil Spector, Lena Horne, Tom Bradley, Vanessa Williams, Nigel Grainge, Chris Hill, Vanessa Redgrave, James Beard, Randolph Scott, Karima Shaw, Leon Haywood, Sanchez Chapman, Denny Bruce, Jerry Boulding, Don Covay, Ron Toussaint, Julian Earls, Robert DeNiro, Chris Blackwell, Bob Fitzpatrick, Calvin Rhodes, Marshall Sehorn, Mary Tyler Moore, Durie Purvis, "Boogaloo" Frazier, Bob Scherl, Eddie Singleton, Farrah Fawcett, William Smith, Burt Reynolds, Jimi Hendrix, Randy Turrow, Bud Cort, Ruby Andrews, Jim Walsh, Mary Ellen, Jeffrey, Jason, Charlie Whitehead, Ruth Brown, Zenobia Earls, Bob Jones, Guitar Shorty, Sharon Liebowitz, Marge Roker, Dick Blackburn, Rick Abrahamson, Sam Watkins (father-in-law), Sue Burke, Steve Brown, Curtis Jordan, Chuck Rush, Paulette De Souza, Roger Curley, Henry Marx, Scott Cameron, Gene Sculatti, Duane Goldberg, Spud, Jeff Grinstein, Pat Speers, Gwen Lanier, Larkin Kennedy, Alison Taylor, Ralph Brickers, Norman Russell, Tommy Hunt, John Goddard, Jeannie Patterson, Val Shivley, Henry Stone, Leland Rogers, Bunky Sheppard, Billy Vera, Gregory Cook, Jerry Peterson, Lee Thornberg, Ed Wright, Elgin Walker, Jamie Webber, Tyrone Davis, and Al Pacino.

Swamp Dogg
Swamp Dogg

SINCE YOU MENTIONED SALT...

In this cookbook you will not find any references to salt as an ingredient in my recipes... nevertheless it is your option and elective. I haven't used it in any of my culinary efforts since 1971... the "year of the great blood-pressure rising." It was higher than giraffe pussy (240 over 180), thus leaving me with no more use for salts and sodiums. I plan to live to write another cookbook, and I'd really be honored if you'd hang around to read and experience it.

3-12-66

Most Promising Duo

1. Sam & Dave (Stax)
2. Sam & Bill (Joda)
3. Sugar Pie De Santo & Etta James (Cadet)

Top Instrumental Combo

1. Jr. Walker & All Stars (Soul)
2. The Packers (Pure Soul)
3. The Mar-Keys (Stax)
4. Booker T & The MGs (Stax)

Most Promising Male Vocalist

1. Jackie Lee (Mirwood)

Bobby Bland (Duke)

2. Deon Jackson (Carla)
3. Eddie Holman (Parkway)
4. Darrow Fletcher (Groovy)
5. Roy Head (Back Beat/Scepter)
6. Edwin Starr (Ric Tic)
7. Little Jerry Williams (Calla)

LITTLE JERRY

WHORES D'OEUVRES WHORES D'OEUVRES WHORES D'OEUVRES WHORES D'OEUVRES

DEVIL WENT DOWN TO GEORGIA FOR EGGS

Even though this is a take on the Charlie Daniels platinum classic, I felt it was more than apropos because my introduction to deviled eggs was via my grandmother, Georgia. I can imagine everyone from Beelzebub to Diogenes searching out and meeting in Georgia's kitchen to gorge on this delicacy.

- *6 eggs*
- *1 quart water*
- *2 tbsp. mayonnaise*
- *1 tbsp. pickle relish*
- *1 very small onion*
- *⅛ tsp. pepper*
- *paprika*
- *pinch sweet basil*
- *pinch rosemary, parsley, and tarragon*

- Place eggs in a 2-quart sauce pan with 1 quart of cold water. Bring to a boil, reduce heat, and cook for 20 minutes. Remove from stove and run cold water over eggs, then set eggs in the freezer for 15 minutes. Peel eggs, cut in half, remove the yellow, and put in a bowl with mayonnaise and pickle relish. Dice onion and add with pepper, basil, rosemary, parsley, and tarragon. Mix all ingredients well. Fill the white egg centers with the egg mixture and sprinkle with paprika.

- Refrigerate, serve cold.

(Serves 4-6)

My grandmother Georgia in uniform... a sergeant most of her life...
Not only did she make the first deviled eggs I ever ate but the best.
She loved me too and I loved her back.

MXR
OTARI

PÂTÉ QUINCY JONES

Pick up any album by Quincy and the credits will be a vast cross section of top musicians, sidemen and featured vocalists, all gathered by Q to satisfy a preponderance of musical taste. My pâté contains the best ingredients right down to the coup de maître, a generous amount of cognac (I use Rémy Martin). Once all of these ingredients come together for a common goal, your taste buds will be chanting "We Are the World."

- *1½ lbs. cooked (boiled) boneless skinned chicken*
- *½ lb. cooked pork*
- *½ lb. cooked ham*
- *1 tbsp. minced garlic*
- *4 scallions (chopped fine)*
- *1 large onion (chopped fine)*
- *2 tbsp. parsley flakes*
- *1 bay leaf*
- *½ tsp. thyme*
- *½ tsp. pepper*
- *2 eggs (beaten)*
- *1 tbsp. flour*
- *½ cup soft butter*
- *¼ cup cognac*
- *½ lb. bacon*

- Chop the chicken, ham, and pork into small pieces. Add garlic, scallions, onions, parsley, bay leaf, thyme, and pepper. Add the butter, eggs, flour, and cognac to this concoction, and stir well until blended. Line a 2-quart casserole with half the bacon, placing the bacon so that it will cover both sides as well as the bottom of casserole. Add the mixture, smooth the top with the back of a spoon or your hands, then top with the remaining bacon, spread over the top. Cover the casserole, place in a pan of hot water, and bake in oven at 350 degrees for 1¼ hours.

- Remove, turn out on a platter, slice and serve on large chunks of French bread.

(Serves 8-12 depending on the rapaciousness of your guests)

FOR THE WEEK OF MARCH 18, 1963

MIGHTY MO'S MIGHTY THIRTY

This Week	Title	Artist
1	Loving You	The Shepherds
2	Tell Daddy	Ben E. King
3	Chapel On The Hill	Little Jerry
4	How Can I Forget	Jimmy Holiday
5	Our Day Will Come	Ruby & The Romantics
6	I Want Her To Love Me	The Larks
7	Let Me Go The Right Way	The Supremes
8	I'm The One Who Loves You	The Impressions
9	Laughlin' Boy	Mary Wells
10	Two Stupid Feet	The Tabs
11	Lonely Soldier	Bobby John
12	Empty Place	Dionne Warwick
13	Good Rockin'	Jr. Walker & All
14	Rainbow	Gene Chandler
15	Contract On Love	Stevie Wonder
16	I'll Make It Alright	The Valentinos
17	Hitch Hike	Marvin Gaye
18	Ask Me	Maxine Brown
19	Fools Rush In	The Hornets
20	Mama Didn't Lie	The Fascinati
21	When You Wish Upon A Star	The Cresents
22	Shook Up Over You	Dee Clark
23	Love Me	The Hornets
24	Moonlight And Music	Ruby & The R
25	That's The Way Love Is	Bobby Bland
26	Up On The Roof	The Drifters
27	Every Day	The Challeng
28	How Do I Stand Today	King & The S
29	Jookin'	Noble Watts
30	I'm Yours	Hoagy Land

JUNIOR JOCKEY OF THE MONTH 10:00

Kay Moulder - Euclid High School

You Get The Number On

JOCKEY JOHN SHOW
2:00 - 6:00p.m.

MR. C's SOULVILLE
12: midnight - 6:00a.m.

KEN HAWKINS - FL
6:00 - 9:30a.m. 12:00

ERNIE'S SIZZLING SOUNDS

By ERNIE DURHAM, WJLB, Detroit

1. The Pain Grows a Little Deeper—Darrow Fletcher
2. You're My Everything—Little Jerry Williams
3. Just One More Day—Otis Redding
4. This Can't Be True—Eddie Holman
5. You Don't Know Like I Know—Sam & Dave
6. For My Baby—The Daylighters
7. Get Out Of My Life Woman—Lee Dorsey
8. For You—The Spellbinders
9. Goodnight My Love—Ben E. King
10. Midnight Affair—Jimmy Hughes

PICKS TO BE CLICKS

Johnny My Boy—The Ad Libs
I Can't Get Away—Bobby Garett
Ooh Baby—Harold Hopkins
Is The Feeling Still There—The Remarkables

Little Eddie Taylor (A Good Buddy)

O.V. WRIGHT, ME, LEON WEN, SIR JOHN HOTEL (Miami) 1966

BREAKFAST
BREAKFAST
BREAKFAST
BREAKFAST
BREAKFAST
BREAKFAST
BREAKFAST
BREAKFAST

SWAMP DOGG'S WAFFLES
ERNIE LEANER

I thought I was kicking ass with my waffles until Ernie came into my kitchen and gave me a few lessons. Now I'm kicking ass!

Ernie Leaner was one of Chicago's big success stories. Ernie opened the first black-owned record distribution company, United Distributors, and built it into a multi-million dollar business. And that was only the beginning. He later founded One-derful, Mar-V-Lus, and Toddlin' Town Records. These labels became the springboard for Alvin Cash, Betty Everett, Bull and the Matadors, Harold Burrage, The Five Du-Tones, McKinley Mitchell, Otis Clay, and about fifty others.

There's much more to be said for my dear friend (now deceased) and I think I will be writing his life story. Which you'll love-because Ernie did it all at least once.

- *2 cups all-purpose flour*
- *1 tbsp. baking powder*
- *1 tsp. sugar*
- *1½ cups milk*
- *4 egg yolks (save whites)*
- *3 tbsp. melted butter*
- *1 tsp. vanilla*

- Grease waffle iron generously with shortening and preheat.

- Combine flour, baking powder, and sugar in a bowl. Add egg yolks to milk. Beat batter by hand until it is semi-smooth but still lumpy. Now add melted butter and vanilla. Beat another 15 strokes. Whip egg whites until fluffy and thick, then fold into batter. Place batter in measuring cup or any other apparatus you have on hand that has a pouring spout. Spread into waffle iron by pouring from middle across each side. Waffles are done when indicated on waffle iron or when top of waffle has risen and a golden-brown waffle is in view, or when steaming stops.

(Serves 4)

Phyllis White... Yvonne's ex-best friend and my ex-good buddy. One day she decided that her life was overcrowded and some would have to get off and wait for the next bus. We did. Shit happens!

Ernie Leaner was always in my kitchen making it smell great.

Charlie Whitehead... eating God knows who or what..........

Herb Cossack, Me, Charlie Whitehead, Bob.... "the party" 74'... home in

Hempstead, L.I.

EGGS CHARLIE WHITEHEAD

How can I acquaint you with Charlie Whitehead in a few short paragraphs? For starters, he's a hell of a songwriter and we collaborated on Dee Dee Warwick's Grammy-nominated "She Didn't Know (She Kept On Talking)" and Travis Wammack's 1975 smash "Love Being Your Fool," which was also a hit on Island Records for Charlie himself.

I produced Charlie when he went by the name Raw Spitt on Canyon Records, and I produced him as himself on Musicor, Sweetheart, Island, United Artists, Wizard, Fungus, and Stone Dogg Records. There were people in the industry who actually thought Charlie was just another pseudonym of mine even though we don't sound anything alike. I loved producing him, writing with him and being his friend.

Charlie is down to earth, home-spun, and talks in parables. A number of our songs were a spinoff of some of his conversations. He's basic... that's why he's Eggs Charlie Whitehead. If you ever meet him, you'll like him and if you never get the pleasure, you will have missed a highlight.

When we were living in Hempstead, Long Island, Charlie used to have a habit of coming to the house and going into the refrigerator and helping himself... which was fine. But one afternoon I walked into the kitchen and Charlie was sitting there, eating like a motherfucker... I said, "Charlie, where did you get that?"... "It was sitting in the front in this red bowl, I heated it... why? Is it yours?" "No, you crazy motherfucker, that's George's food!"... George was the dog and the food was a combination of scraps and ALPO. Charlie continued eating. "It's good," he said. "And if it won't kill the dog it won't kill me."

If you're ever in Brooklyn go see him perform. He possesses a soul and delivery much like that of Al Green... except he doesn't sound like Al Green.

- *bacon (8 strips)*
- *8 tbsp. chili sauce*
- *8 eggs*
- *8 tsp. butter (melted)*
- *paprika*
- *8 pineapple slices (drained)*
- *parsley*

- Preheat oven to 325 degrees.

- In a frying pan, sauté bacon lightly. Grease 8 muffin-pan cups. Line the sides of each cup with a strip of bacon. Put in 1 tbsp. of chili sauce, crack and drop 1 egg in each cup, and top with 1 tsp. of melted butter. Sprinkle with paprika to taste. Put in oven and bake for 10 minutes and turn onto pineapple slices with a spoon. Garnish each one with parsley.

(Serves 4)

Williams Signed In Three Posts At Musicor Records

NEW YORK—Jerry Williams will be working at Musicor in the triple-positions of singer, producer and writer for the label's Catalogue publishing affiliate.

First release from the pop-r&b artist as a performer will be the Musicor single "Run Run Roadrunner." His production talent will be used for both the Musicor and Dynamo labels.

Williams has previously been involved in productions for the Orlons, Bobby Peterson, Freddy Cannon and recent jobs with Calla, Loma and Aldo Records.

Cashbox — 11-11-67

R&B SPOTLIGHTS

TOP 10 Spotlights—Predicted to reach the TOP SELLING RHYTHM & BLUES SINGLES Chart

LEON HAYWOOD — MELLOW MOONLIGHT (Prod. Leon Haywood) (Writer: Haywood) **(Eve-jim, BMI)**—His "It's Gotta Be Mellow" proved a giant on the r&b chart and rode up the Hot 100 as well. This blockbuster blues rocker should push him farther up both charts. Electrifying performance. Flip: "Tennessee Waltz" (Acuff-Rose, BMI). **Decca 32230**

INEZ & CHARLIE FOXX—(1,2,3,4,5,6,7) COUNT THE DAYS (Prod. Charlie Foxx) (Writers: Williams-Foxx-Williams) **(Catalogue/Cee & Eye, BMI)**—A wild and wailing easy-beat rocker that can't miss climbing right up to the top part of the r&b chart in short order. Grooves all the way through. Flip: "A Stranger I Don't Know" (Vee Vee/Cee & Eye, BMI) **Dynamo 112**

GENE CHANDLER—NO PEACE, NO SATISFACTION (Prod. Carl Davis) (Writers: Butler-Griffin) **(Jalynne, BMI)**—That "To Be a Lover" wailer has another sure-fire winner in this pulsating rocker that never quits from start to finish. Should prove a Hot 100 item as well. Flip: "I Won't Need You" (Jalynne, BMI). **Checker 1190**

NOVEMBER 25, 1967, BILLBOARD

Williams Joins Musicor

Jerry Williams, a singer in the pop-R&B school, has joined Musicor Records, according to Stanley Kahan, Director of Artists and Repertoire.

Williams will also operate as a writer for the Musicor-affiliated Catalogue Music firm and as a producer for both Musicor and the affiliated Dynamo label.

RECORD WORLD—November 11, 1967

Private Swamp Dogg....8/64, Ft. Jackson, S.C. Drafted 10/1/64, honorably discharged 8 days later, 10/8/64... remind me to tell you the story of bureaucracy.

BEANS BEANS BEANS BEANS BEANS

JOE TURNER BEANS
BOOGIE WOOGIE COUNTRY GIRL

"Boogie Woogie Country Girl" was one of Joe Turner's big hits. I never missed an appearance by him when he came through Portsmouth, and he was always headlining the show. I even tried to sing like him, which I couldn't do because my voice wasn't low enough. It never did get low enough, but I still sing a couple of his songs. Everything he did, I loved. I don't know. I guess I was a groupie for him or some shit.

- *1 lb. baby white limas*
- *1 tsp. black pepper*
- *2 tsp. salt*
- *½ tsp. of baking soda*
- *½ tsp. of minced garlic*
- *1 small onion quartered*
- *1 cooked hambone (one you have left over in the freezer from your last big family affair with some lean/fat remaining)*
- *4 qts. water*
- *½ slice canned pineapple*

- Pick and wash the beans and place in a large pot with all the ingredients. Cover and cook over a low flame for 1½ hours. Remove the pineapple and cook 2 hours more or until the beans are tender.

- Why baking soda? It eliminates 75% of the backlash (farts).

- This dish is so good it'll make you slap your mama... among other people.

(6-8 generous servings)

BIG JOE TURNER

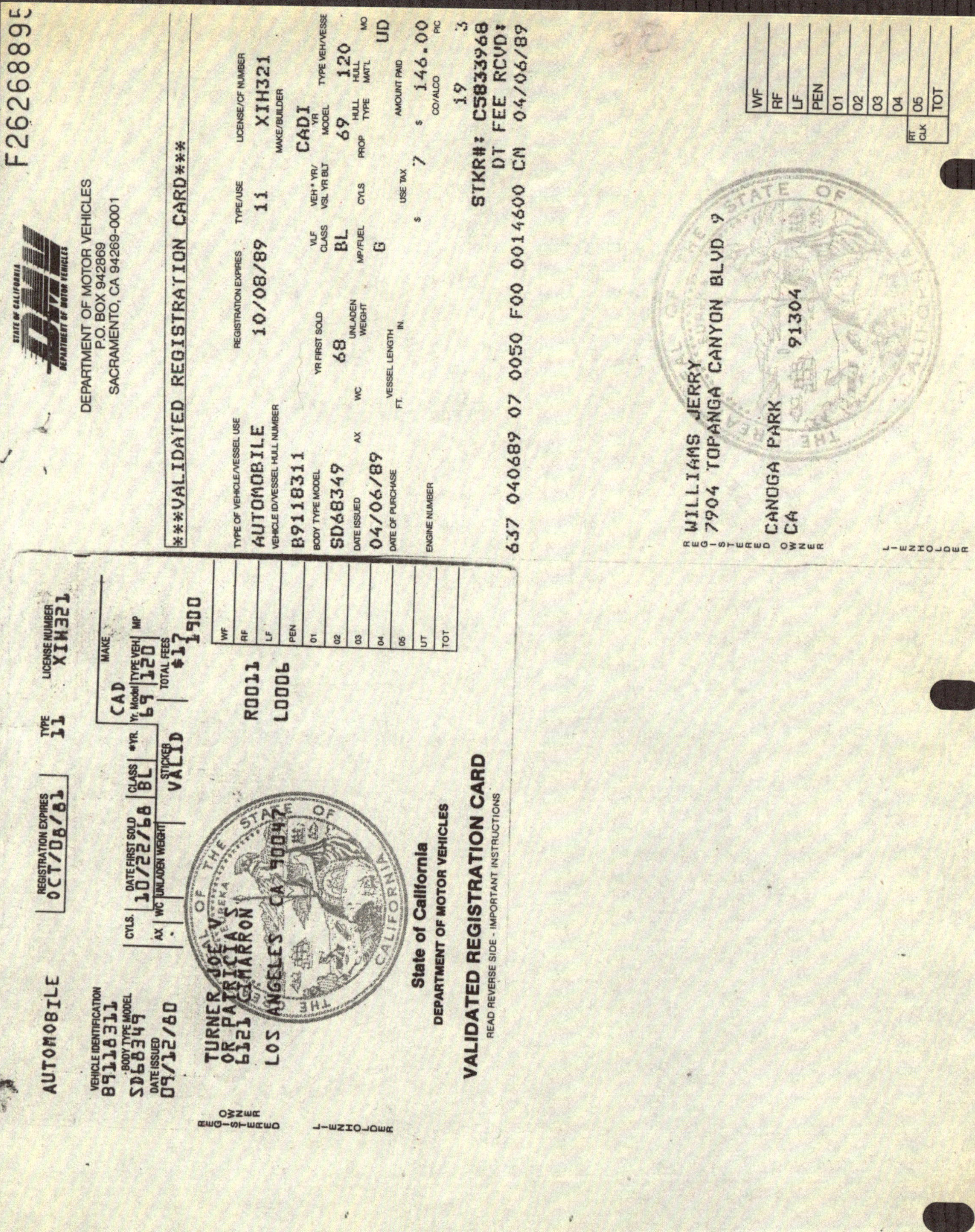

F26268895

STATE OF CALIFORNIA DMV DEPARTMENT OF MOTOR VEHICLES

DEPARTMENT OF MOTOR VEHICLES
P.O. BOX 942869
SACRAMENTO, CA 94269-0001

VALIDATED REGISTRATION CARD

TYPE OF VEHICLE/VESSEL USE: AUTOMOBILE
REGISTRATION EXPIRES: 10/08/89
TYPE/USE: 11
LICENSE/CF NUMBER: XIH321
VEHICLE ID/VESSEL HULL NUMBER: B9118311
MAKE/BUILDER: CADI
BODY TYPE MODEL: SD68349
YR FIRST SOLD: 68
VLF CLASS: BL
VEH YR: 69
TYPE VEH: 120
DATE ISSUED: 04/06/89
MP/FUEL: G
MO: UD
USE TAX: $ 7
AMOUNT PAID: $ 146.00
CO/ALCO: 19
PIC: 3

637 040689 07 0050 F00 0014600 CN
STKR#: C5833968
DT FEE RCVD: 04/06/89

REGISTERED OWNER:
WILLIAMS JERRY
7904 TOPANGA CANYON BLVD 9
CANOGA PARK
CA 91304

LIENHOLDER

WF RF LF PEN 01 02 03 04 05 TOT

AUTOMOBILE

VEHICLE IDENTIFICATION: B9118311
BODY TYPE MODEL: SD68349
DATE ISSUED: 09/12/80
REGISTRATION EXPIRES: OCT/08/81
DATE FIRST SOLD: 10/22/68
CLASS: BL
STICKER: VALID
TYPE: 11
LICENSE NUMBER: XIH321
MAKE: CAD
YR. MODEL: 69
TYPE VEH: 120
TOTAL FEES: $17 1900

R0011
L0006

REGISTERED OWNER:
TURNER JOE V
OR PATRICIA S
6121 CIMARRON
LOS ANGELES CA 90047

LIENHOLDER

State of California
DEPARTMENT OF MOTOR VEHICLES
VALIDATED REGISTRATION CARD
READ REVERSE SIDE - IMPORTANT INSTRUCTIONS

I had to have his favorite cadillac after his passing as a rememberance and symbol of what he meant to me. His music helped shape my musical style and the piano stylings of his longtime musical partner, Pete Johnson can still be heard in snatches in a number of my recordings.

ST. LOUIS BLACKEYE PEA BLUES

Don't cover these little troublemakers with water or bring to a boil and let them stand. If you do, you'll become a victim of their blues. You'll be blowing evergreens out your ass by W.C. Handy, Parliament-Funkadelic, and many more. So follow the fuckin' recipe.

- *1 lb. blackeye peas*
- *2 onions (quartered)*
- *4 large or 6 medium ham hocks (cracked)*
- *1 tsp. garlic powder*
- *1 tbsp. black pepper*
- *1 tsp. chili powder*
- *2 tbsp. ketchup*

- Pour blackeye peas on a plate or countertop and pick out all the bad peas (brown, bruised, etc.). Put the peas in a colander and rinse. Cover with water in a large pot and bring to a boil, remove from heat and let stand for 1 hour. In a 4-quart pot place the ham hocks, onions, garlic powder, pepper, chili powder, and ketchup. Cover with water, bring to a boil, reduce to low heat, and cover. Add peas to pot, cover, and continue to cook until done, approximately 3 hours.

- Serve over rice with sliced tomatoes and cornbread.

(Makes 4-6 el grande servings)

BAKED-BEANS BO DIDDLEY

Bo Diddley has always mesmerized and amazed me with his weird-ass songs, weird looking guitars, and Africa-meets-Chicago musical grooves. Bo used to always play the Capitol Theatre in Portsmouth, Virginia, with his real weird looking maracas player, Jerome Greene, who reminded me of one flying over the cuckoo.

Bo introduced fun into rhythm 'n' blues, which is why I dedicated a dish to him that's usually prevalent at fun-filled events and holidays.

I approached Bo about eight years ago regarding me producing him and placing him with a label. After listening to his twenty-minute retort on his greatness, his sheriffing in New Mexico, and who the fuck am I, I felt like something he'd eliminated from his ass. One day I'll learn how to be a devoted fan and stay the hell out of harm's way.

- *1 32 oz. can pork 'n' beans*
- *4 tbsp. butter*
- *½ cup brown sugar (old fashioned or light brown)*
- *2 tbsp. flour (browned)*
- *4 tbsp. water*
- *1 tbsp. grated orange peel*
- *3 tbsp. dark heavy corn syrup*

- Melt butter over low heat in a heavy frying pan. Add brown sugar to melted butter and cook for 5 minutes or until butter and sugar become thick and sticky. Combine flour and water with pork 'n' beans. Add beans to fry pan mixture and stir. Sprinkle orange peel over beans. Remove from stove and place in 350-degree oven for ½ hour uncovered. Pour syrup over beans and return to oven for 10 minutes.

- Remove and cool for 10 minutes.

(Serves 8)

December 1965 – "Baby, You're My Everything" – no 1 in N.Y.

KEEP THIS — IT IS A REMINDER OF GREAT SHOWS TO COME

AT THE **APOLLO THEATRE** 125 STREET Nr. 8th AVE.

TOMMY SMALLS PRESENTS-**ONE WEEK** Beg. **FRI. DEC. 24th**

SOLOMON BURKE

The SHIRELLES

CHARLIE & INEZ FOXX

SAM & DAVE

PAUL KELLY "CHILLS and FEVER"

Little JERRY WILLIAMS "YOU'RE MY EVERYTHING"

4 TELEVISION SETS GIVEN AWAY (FREE) LAST SHOW XMAS EVE

ONE WEEK Beg..... FRIDAY DEC. 31st

THE **GREATEST BLUES** *SINGERS IN THE* **WORLD**

BO DIDDLEY SEXTET

MUDDY WATERS

JOHN LEE HOOKER

T-BONE WALKER

BETTY CARTER

SONNY TERRY & BROWNIE McGEE

JEAN DUSHON

SPO DEE O DEE-COMIC

HERMAN AMIS- M.C.

1650 Broadway, Suite 1211, New York, N.Y. 10019 Tel: 757-

BOTANIC
RECORDS INC.

JERRY WILLIAMS, JR.
A & R Director

BROOKS & JERRY

John Philip Soul with a vocal version, also on the Atlantic-distributed Dakar label. . . . Wayne Cochran . . . blue-eyed . . . will appear at the Fillmore East rock house the weekend of Feb. 6-7. . . . Atlantic has signed independent producer **Jerry Williams Jr.** to its staff. Williams, who was formerly with Botanic Records and Musicor, was also signed as a singer and will debut with "Shipwreck" on the Cotillion label. . . . Wilson will be . . . the "Tonight" . . . replacing Johnny Carson from Feb. 3-7. . . . **Clarence Carter** will appear in Freeport, Bahamas, and Nassau Jan. 24-27. . . . **C and the Shells,** formerly

(Continued on page 37)

JANUARY 11, 1969, BILLBOARD

SOUL SAUCE

Continued from page 36

the **Sand Pebbles** ("Love Power") have been signed by Gate Artist Management and Universal Attractions for bookings. They have also signed with Atlantic and will be produced by **Jerry Williams, Jr.,** also a newcomer to the staff as an inside producer. . . . Bay Sound Records in Baltimore is supplying the city with local . . . the **Bleu Lights'** "Yes I Do.". . . **Aretha Franklin** was named the top female singer of Finland. . . . The **Supremes** have five LP's on the R&B charts and two singles. . . . The **Sweet Inspirations** were awarded a gold record at Carnegie Hall for their background harmonizing on over 300 disks—and **Aretha Franklin's** "I Say a Little Prayer.". . . **Jerry Wexler** of Atlantic Records reads **Soul Sauce.** Do you?

Billboard 1-4-69

Executive Turntable

HARPER

Herman Harper has been added to the Don Light Talent Agency, Nashville, as general manager. He was a singer with the **Oak Ridge Boys** for several years. . . . **C. J. (Red) Gentry,** former radio products manager of Motorola, has been named product manager, automotive products of the consumer products division of the firm. Gentry has been with Motorola 18 years. He'll report to **C. Vernon Phillips,** manager, radio and audio products. . . . **Jerry Williams Jr.** has been signed as a producer and recording artist for Atlantic Records. He'd been vice-president and a&r director of Botanic Records and before that a producer, writer, artist with Musicor Records. First release as artist will be "Shipwreck" on Atlantic's Cotillion label.

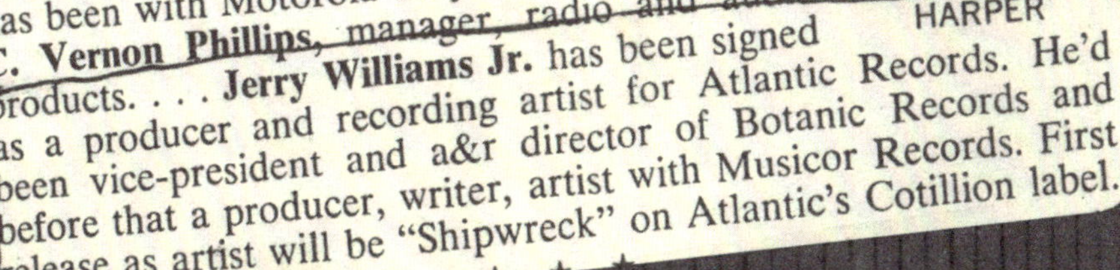

Cashbox..1/4/69

Jerry Williams To Atl.

NEW YORK—Jerry Williams, Jr., most recently a vice president and A&R director with Botanic Records, has joined Atlantic Records in the dual role of artist and producer.

Before his tenure with Botanic, Williams was a producer, writer and artist with Musicor Records, where he wrote and arranged "Count The Days," the recent Inez and Charlie Foxx hit and co-produced Gene Pitney's "She's A Heartbreaker" with Foxx. While with Botanic, Williams produced the Gary "U.S." Bonds record, "I'm Glad You're Back" and others.

BEEF BEEF BEEF BEEF

T-BONE (STEAK) WALKER

B.B. King, Albert King, Freddy King, and King Hussein are just a few superstars who credit T-Bone Walker for how they play and sing the blues. He was a star in the 1940s and '50s. Aaron T-Bone Walker introduced unforgettable arpeggios and most of all was the first blues guitarist to use an electric instrument. I used to go see him also at the Capitol Theatre and always walked away dazzled by his artistry and near perfect playing ability, not to mention his impeccable vocals.

When I was growing up, t-bone steak was top-of-the-line eating and T-Bone Walker was top-of-the-line entertainment.

- *4 large sirloin steaks*
- *4 medium-size onions*
- *3 tbsp. soy sauce*
- *1 cup flour*
- *1 tbsp. pepper*
- *1 tbsp. dried parsley flakes*
- *1 tbsp. paprika*
- *1 tsp. Beau Monde*
- *1 cup. bacon fat*
- *1 green pepper chopped*
- *6 tbsp. Worcestershire sauce*
- *2 cups milk*
- *1 cup water*

- Cut steak into 2-inch cubes. Combine flour, pepper, parsley, paprika, and Beau Monde, then dredge the steak in the mixture. In a Dutch oven, pour bacon fat, heat and add steak, onions, green peppers, soy sauce, and Worcestershire sauce. Cook over low heat until all ingredients are ¾ done. Add milk and water and continue to simmer until done, about 2 hours over low heat.

(Serves 6-8)

MAMBO CLUB

MATINEE

SUN. AFTERNOON

MAR. 23rd

TIME: 2 p.m. to 7 p.m.

$1.75 ADVANCE $2.00 AT DOOR

Direction-Overton & Nicholson=Wichita, Kansas

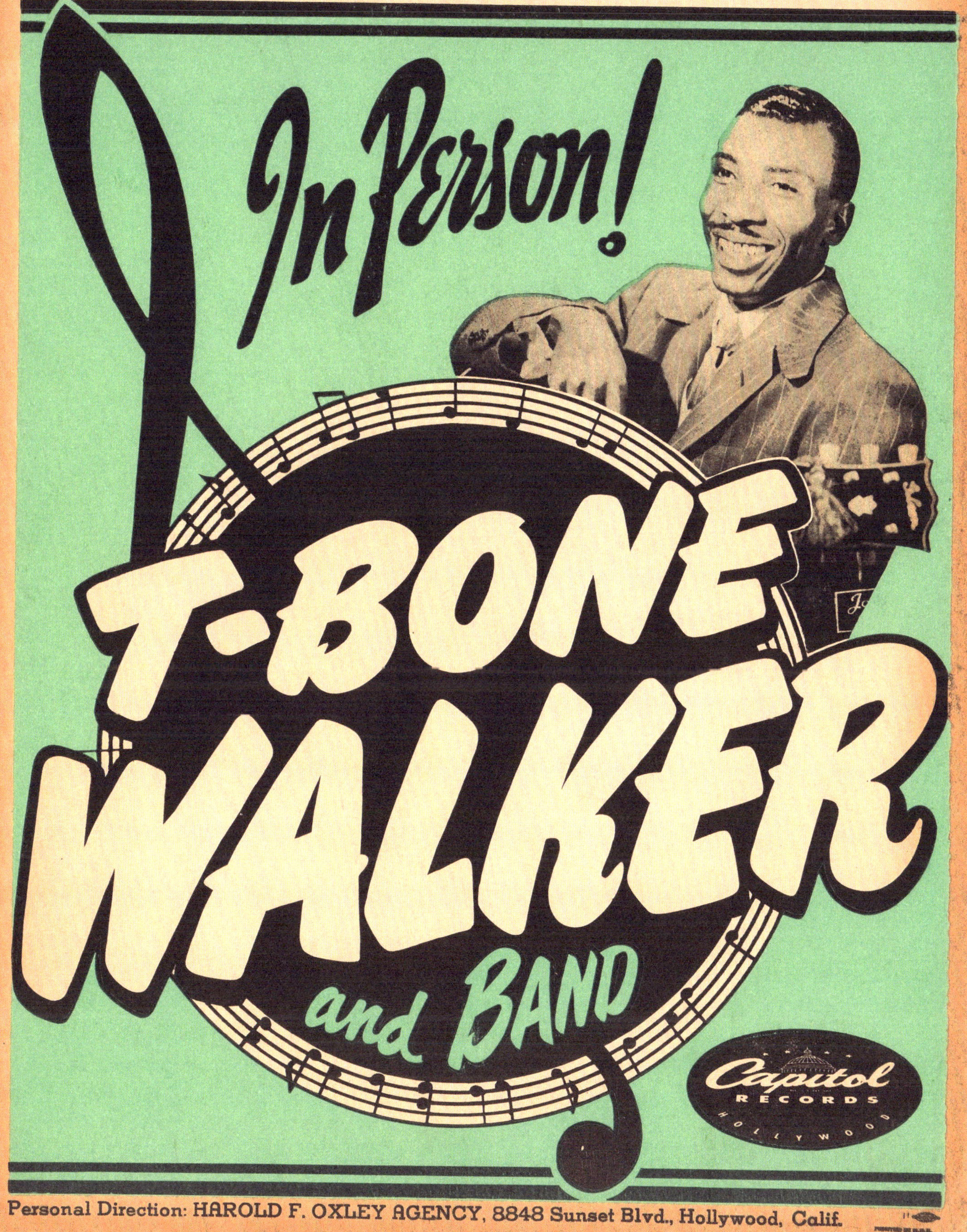

B.B. KING CROWN ROAST

This dedication is self-explanatory.

- *crown roast of beef (5-7 lbs.)*
- *1 green pepper sliced*
- *1 onion quartered*
- *1 tsp. garlic powder*
- *⅓ cup cognac (top shelf unnecessary/ bottom shelf out of the question)*

- Place roast on a sheet of aluminum foil (shiny side down). Sprinkle roast with garlic and garnish with onion and green peppers. Place in a preheated oven at 300 degrees for 1 hour. Remove from oven and saturate with cognac. Replace foil and place back in oven for 1½ hours more.

(Serves 6-8)

HANK WILLIAMS JR. CHEESE STEAK SANDWICH

I love every record Hank Jr. made after he left MGM records, and that's why I named this dish after him. I also was hoping that with us being namesakes, Hank Sr. might have sired me on the other side of the fence, thus giving me a shot at some of that Acuff-Rose publishing monies earned by "Cold Cold Heart" and about three hundred more smash hits. Hi brother Hank, drop me a line... or better still a cashier's check from dad...

- *½ lb. beef round steak (wafer thin)*
- *1 large onion*
- *¼ tsp. pepper*
- *¼ tsp. garlic powder*
- *⅓ tsp. oil*
- *3 long French rolls**
- *3 slices American cheese*
- *2 tbsp. ketchup*

- Slice steak into ½-inch slithers. Slice onions into ¼-inch rings, then separate the rings. Sprinkle pepper and garlic over steak. Heat oil in a skillet over medium heat. Steam rolls. Put steak and onions in skillet and stir till steak is partially brown, add ketchup continue till totally brown. Divide steak and onions in 3 sections in the pan and place 1 piece cheese on each section and place a roll split half open over the steak (about 1 minute).

- Lift out of skillet with a spatula and serve.

* *After splitting roll, gently press the inside down with your thumbs to provide more room for ingredients.*

(Serves 3)

HANK WILLIAMS exclusively on **M-G-M Records**

Billboard...1/11/69

From The Music Capitals of the World

AMSTERDAM

Red Bullet managing director **Fred Haayen** flew to New York to negotiate for the Dutch rights of TV specials by **Diana Ross and the Supremes** and the **Temptations.** . . . Dutch group the **Golden Earrings** have been booked to appear in a special show in Cologne called "Beat, But Not From England" Friday and Saturday (9-10). . . . The 71-piece **Ossipov Ensemble** from Moscow, and **James Last** have been invited to participate in

TOM DOWD, left, an Atlantic-Atco vice-president and recipient of Bill Gavin's R&B Producer of the Year award, reviews sessions for the new year with Jerry Williams Jr., the label's newly signed addition to producing staff.

SWAMP DOGG POLYNESIAN BEEF THINS

Don't ask... Maybe I'm Polynesian... I don't know... The dish is great!

- *1 lb. beef loin tails**
- *1 tsp. minced garlic*
- *½ tsp. pepper*
- *½ tsp. lemon peel grated*
- *1 onion sliced and ringed*
- *1 green pepper sliced and ringed thin*
- *⅔ cup oil*
- *10 oz. can pineapple chunks*

- Slice beef into micro-thin slivers, sprinkle with pepper and grated lemon peel and let stand for 15 minutes. Heat oil over medium flame and add garlic, stir garlic for 10 seconds, add green peppers and beef (cook covered for 5 minutes). Stir and add onions and pineapple chunks, cover (cook 5 minutes more). Uncover and stir constantly for 5 minutes more.

- Serve over rice or fried noodles.

* *It is most important that beef is sliced micro-thin or it will be tough to talk about.*

(Serves 5)

CORNED BEEF CHA CHA CHA

I'd love to be able to tie corned beef and the Cha Cha Cha together, but I can't, other than to say I like the way they verbalize. No matter how fast or slow you say it, the Cha Cha Cha always has a singing sound. Say it... Say it real fast... I told you...

- *4-5 lbs. corned-beef brisket*
- *1 tsp. pepper*
- *4 yellow onions (halved)*
- *1 lb. sweet Italian sausage*
- *6 carrots (cut into 1-inch pieces)*
- *1 clove of garlic (chopped)*
- *6 white potatoes peeled and cut in half*
- *2 green peppers (quartered)*
- *12 oz. can whole kernel corn*
- *1 lb. 12 oz. can tomatoes*
- *1 head cabbage (cut into 6 wedges)*
- *1 lb. can chickpeas*
- *2 stalks celery with leaves cut in 4-inch pieces*

- Place corned beef in a large heavy pot covered with water. Add pepper, onions, and sausage. Cover and bring to a boil, then reduce heat and simmer for 2½ hours. Put in the remaining ingredients and simmer another 45 minutes. Drain off the broth and pour in to a bowl. Serve the broth in 8 oz. cups, then slice the beef and serve with the vegetables.

(Makes 5-7 servings)

ニュー秋葉原センター
シャープ
シントク
SHINTOKU
2F
1F
中華・お食事
健康預金
お取扱中
ボーナスは
当店へ
SHINTOKU
SONY
無線
家電製品
TAX FREE

Fungus Finder In the Yen

WWRL program director Enoch Gregory might as well have reached across the sea when he reached into the "fungus bag" to draw the winning entry in BASF Records' recent contest to guess the name of its new r&b label—Fungus. Of the many correct guesses, Gregory drew the entry of Yoichi Maeda of Minato-Ku, Tokyo who will receive nearly thirteen thousand Yen, or five hundred American dollars at current exchange rates. With Gregory (from left) Norma Pinelli, music director of WWRL; BASF and Fungus sales and promotion manager Herb Heldt and Mrs. Jerry (Yvonne) Williams, wife of the "Swamp Dog" man who produced the label's initial sides.

TUBE STEAKS WARREN LANIER

"Hello, Lanier Media"... that's how you'll be greeted if you dial 818-386-2790. Warren is my dear, dear friend, a Gemini, and a public relations man, in that order. He's the answer for all P.R. needs... whether it's a tournament, play, recording, film, novel, whatever.

Warren and I have a partiality for these hot dogs that you buy from those vendors on the streets of Manhattan, who should have been condemned by the health department years ago.

Where do they wash their hands? How did those gloves they wear with the fingers cut out get so goddamn nasty? Where do they relieve themselves? In that dirty ass bucket they have hanging from the cart? I hope these unanswered questions do not hold the clue to the incomplete succulence of their dogs. When they top your dog with those onions and you bite into it you can feel the earth move like it did with your first cognizant organism, and the Wolfgang Pucks of the world all seem to be amateurs.

I quickly learned how to duplicate the onions, steam the roll, and use Nathan's hot dogs, and believe me Warren goes crazy. He has eaten it all and I mean all (let your imagination soar) yet he keeps this at the top of his "must have often" list.

To the man who produced, discovered, and almost lost his mind managing Leon Haywood, Etta Jones, and The Rivieras, I dedicate my hot dog.

Anyone who's ever met him would never guess that Warren a.k.a The Black Prince is a "sho nuf" country boy hailing from Criss Country, Georgia, because he is slick dressing, slick talking, and silky smooth... especially after a magnum of his bubbly.

- Recipe? It's a hot dog, you can figure it out yourself.

MEATLOAF LITTLE MILTON

For the six of you who don't know, Little Milton is a blues legend who would be a B.B. King-type superstar if blacks supported the blues the way white people do.

I've known Milton since '67 but I didn't get a chance to experiment on his palate until 1989. I prepared this meatloaf and he loved it, which wasn't difficult since we were washing it down with Rémy Martin.

Here's to you Milton.

- *1 lb. ground beef*
- *1 10oz. can tomato soup*
- *1 egg (beaten)*
- *⅔ cup bread or cracker crumbs*
- *½ tsp. crushed red pepper*
- *1 tbsp. parsley flakes (dried)*
- *1 tbsp. dried chopped onions*
- *¼ tsp. nutmeg*
- *½ tsp. sugar*
- *2 strips bacon*

- In a large bowl, combine all ingredients with the exception of bacon. Mix well, spoon into a baking dish, and pat into a loaf. Lay the bacon strips across the top of the loaf. Place dish in oven and bake 1 hour at 350 degrees.

(Serves 4-6)

Paul Hornsby at the keys

Nat Cross, the father who raised me. Piano, guitar, bass, drums, accordian, assorted horns... a musician's musician

adidas

TONE LOC MEATLOAF

This rapper/actor always looks to me like a six-foot meatloaf with human abilities. Oh yes, I love his albums, but when my wife started raving about him as he emerged on the scene with "Wild Thing," I thought she was just as crazy as he was bad. Nevertheless, after hearing this record every day, twenty times a day, I started comparing it to Smokey Robinson's "Tracks of My Tears."

This recipe is dedicated with love and respect.

- *1½ lbs. lean ground beef*
- *1 10¾oz. can tomato soup*
- *1 tsp. crushed red pepper*
- *15 Spanish olives sliced thin*
- *1 tsp. minced garlic*
- *1 tbsp. parsley flakes*
- *1 tbsp. chopped chives*
- *2 eggs beaten*
- *1 tbsp. basil*
- *½ tsp. tarragon leaves*

- Preheat oven to 350 degrees.

- Mix all ingredients together in a large bowl. Place in a 4-by-8-by-4-inch dish or pan and shape into a loaf. Bake for 55 minutes.

(Serves 8)

BEST SELLING

Billboard Rhythm & Blues Singles

Billboard SPECIAL SURVEY For Week Ending 5/10/69

★ STAR Performer—Single's registering greatest proportionate upward progress this week.

This Week	Last Week	Title, Artist, Label, No. & Pub.	Weeks on Chart
1 (Billboard Award)	1	**IT'S YOUR THING** Isley Brothers, T Neck 901 (Brothers Three, BMI)	9
2	2	**CHOKIN' KIND** Joe Simon, Sound Stage 7 2628 (Wilderness, BMI)	7
3	3	**ONLY THE STRONG SURVIVE** Jerry Butler, Mercury 72898 (Parabut/Double Diamond/Downstairs, BMI)	10
4	4	**I DON'T WANT NOBODY TO GIVE ME NOTHING** James Brown, King 6624 (Dynatone, BMI)	5
5	6	**CISSY STRUT** Meters, Josie 45-1005 (Marsaint Music, BMI)	4
★6	8	**AQUARIUS/LET THE SUNSHINE IN** 5th Dimension, Soul City 772 (United Artists, ASCAP)	7
★7	30	**TOO BUSY THINKING ABOUT MY BABY** Marvin Gaye, Tamla 54181 (Jobete, BMI)	2
8	9	**TIME IS TIGHT** Booker T. & the M.G.'s, Stax 0028 (East Memphis, BMI)	6
9	5	**IS IT SOMETHING YOU'VE GOT** Tyrone Davis, Dakar 605 (Dakar, BMI)	7
10	10	**BUYING A BOOK** Joe Tex, Dial 4090 (Tree, BMI)	4
11	13	**I CAN'T SEE MYSELF LEAVING YOU** Aretha Franklin, Atlantic 2619 (14th Hour, BMI)	3
12	7	**RUN AWAY CHILD RUNNING WILD** Temptations, Gordy 7084 (Jobete, BMI)	11
13	11	**DIDN'T YOU KNOW** Gladys Knight & the Pips, Soul 35057 (Jobete, BMI)	8
14	15	**SUNDAY** Moments, Stang 5003 (Gambi, BMI)	5
15	16	**SEVEN YEARS** Impressions, Curtom 1940 (Camed, BMI)	4
★16	37	**JUST A LITTLE BIT** Little Milton, Checker 1217 (Arc, BMI)	3
17	12	**TWENTY-FIVE MILES** Edwin Starr, Gordy 7083 (Jobete, BMI)	12
18	18	**NEVER GONNA LET HIM KNOW** Debbie Taylor, GWP 501 (Willbridge/MRC, BMI)	8
19	17	**DO YOUR THING** Watts 103rd Street Rhythm Band, Reprise 7250 (Wright/Gersti/Tamerlane, BMI)	12
20	21	**GRAZING IN THE GRASS** Friends of Distinction, RCA Victor 74-0207 (Chisa, BMI)	6
21	14	**DON'T TOUCH ME** Bettye Swann, Capitol 2382 (Pamper, BMI)	8
22	24	**WALK AWAY** Ann Peeples, Hi 2157 (Saico/Jec, BMI)	4
★23	32	**STAND** Sly & the Family Stone, Epic 5-10450 (Daly City, BMI)	4
★24	36	**SO I CAN LOVE YOU** Emotions, Volt 4010 (Pervis/Staples, BMI)	2
★25	—	**COMPOSER** Diana Ross & the Supremes, Motown M-1146 (Jobete, BMI)	1
★26	—	**PROUD MARY** Solomon Burke, Bell 783 (Jon Dora, BMI)	1
★27	33	**IT'S A GROOVY WORLD** James Brown, King 6222 (Golo, BMI)	5
★28	41	**WE'VE GOT HONEY LOVE** Martha Reeves & the Vandellas, Gordy 7085 (Jobete, BMI)	3
★29	48	**WE GOT MORE SOUL** Dyke & the Blazers, Original Sound 86 (Drive-In, BMI)	3
★30	39	**I CAN'T SAY NO TO YOU** Betty Everett, UNI 55122 (Screen Gems-Columbia, BMI)	3
31	20	**I CAN'T DO ENOUGH** Dells, Cadet 5636 (Chevis Music, BMI)	7
32	26	**ICE CREAM SONG** Dynamics, Cotillion 44021 (Dlief-Cotillion, BMI)	11
33	34	**IT'S A MIRACLE** Willie Hightower, Capitol 2226 (Too Late Music, BMI)	6
34	28	**YOU ARE THE CIRCUS** C & the Shells, Cotillion 44024 (Cotillion/Williams, BMI)	6
35	27	**ARE YOU LONELY FOR ME BABY** C. Jackson, Motown 1144 (Webb IV, BMI)	4
★36	49	**WHY I SING THE BLUES** B. B. King, BluesWay 61034 (Pamco/Sounds of Lucille, BMI)	2
37	38	**T. C. B. OR T. Y. A.** Bobby Patterson, Jetstar 114 (Jetstar, BMI)	3
38	35	**ANY DAY NOW** Percy Sledge, Atlantic 2616 (Plan Too, ASCAP)	4
39	40	**STUFF** Jeanette Williams, Back Beat 601 (Don, BMI)	3
★40	47	**MY WIFE, MY DOG, MY CAT** Maskmen & the Agents, Dynamo 131 (Catalogue/Clairborne, BMI)	2
41	42	**ME TARZAN, YOU JANE** Intruders, Gamble 225 (Razor Sharp, BMI)	2
42	44	**CRYING IN THE RAIN** Sweet Inspirations, Atlantic 2620 (Screen Gems-Columbia, BMI)	2
43	46	**WHY SHOULD WE STOP NOW** Natural Four, ABC 11205 (Wilhos/Pamco, BMI)	2
★44	—	**JUST A DREAM** Ruby Winters, Diamond 258 (Ace, BMI)	1
★45	—	**(I WANNA) TESTIFY** Johnnie Taylor, Stax 0033 (Groovesville, BMI)	1
★46	—	**I WANT TO LOVE YOU BABY** Peggy Scott & JoJo Benson, SSS International 769 (Green Owl, ASCAP)	1
★47	—	**OH HAPPY DAY** Edwin Hawkins Singers, Buddah 20001 (Kama Rippa/Hawkins, ASCAP)	1
★48	—	**YOU'VE MADE ME SO VERY HAPPY** Blood, Sweat & Tears, Columbia 4-44776 (Jobete, BMI)	1
★49	—	**O WOW** Panic Button, Gamble 230 (Binn/Overlook, ASCAP)	1
★50	—	**GOTTA GET TO KNOW YOU BETTER** Bobby Bland, Duke 447 (Don, BMI)	1

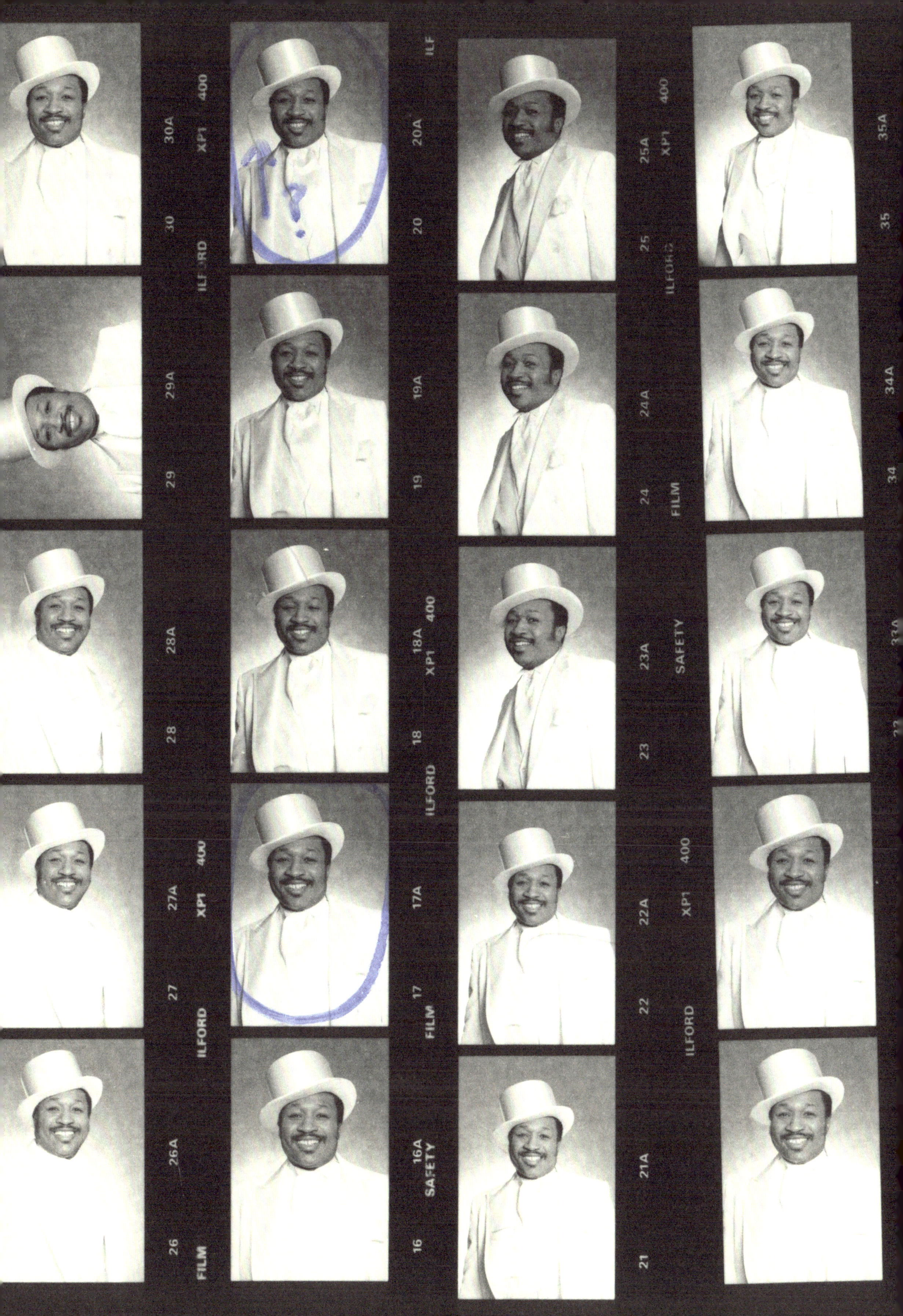

BREADS
BREADS
BREADS
BREADS
BREADS
BREADS

GATES COUNTY BUTTERMILK BISCUITS

Gates County, North Carolina... that's where my great-grands, grands, great aunts, aunts, and cousins, everyone who taught me to cook, hailed from. They migrated to Portsmouth, Virginia, in the early 1900s and took all of their great recipes with them. Biscuits, cornbread, and cakes were among my cooking accomplishments by the time I was nine years old. And since you nor I are aware of anything of any importance or anyone of any repute (other than my family) hailing from Gates County, I feel it only proper that we give this little place a reason for being there. So, I give you Gates County Buttermilk Biscuits.

- *1 tsp. sugar*
- *2 cups all-purpose flour (sifted)*
- *½ tsp. baking powder*
- *¼ tsp. baking soda*
- *½ cup of buttermilk*
- *5 tbsp. melted butter*

- Preheat oven to 450 degrees.

- Combine flour, baking powder, baking soda, and sugar in a bowl. Push all the ingredients to the side, making a well in the center. Pour in the buttermilk, gradually add butter, stir with a fork until the ingredients are nice and moist. Add more milk little by little until the dough is soft and light, not sticky.

- It is impossible to be exact about the amount of milk because flours differ so much. Turn out dough on a floured board. With floured hands pat dough until smooth. Roll into an oblong and cut out biscuits. Place biscuits on a ungreased baking sheet or pan.

- Bake 20 minutes or until golden brown.

(Makes about 9 large biscuits.)

Buddy Scott..says he'll drink anything - just as long as it's wet and he'll eat anything... I don't know whether Buddy is a good gauge or not, other than he cleans his plate.

TEMPTATIONS CORNBREAD

Like millions of others, I loved The Temptations and I dedicate this recipe to them because they summarized my cornbread in their songs when they sang "It's Growing"... which was really about what happens to one's appetite after one slice... just like "Get Ready" is your attitude when you're cognizant of what's in the oven... and "Ain't Too Proud to Beg" is how you feel once you've devoured your slice or slices... and "(I Know) I'm Losing You" names your sentiment when the last existing morsel is being masticated. Of course, "Cloud Nine" is the place everyone feels they've reached as they retire from my dining table.

- *1 cup soft butter*
- *⅓ cup sugar*
- *1 cup flour*
- *1 tbsp. baking powder*
- *1 cup yellow cornmeal*
- *3 eggs (beaten slightly)*
- *1¼ cups milk (room temperature)*
- *¼ cup Monterey Jack cheese diced*
- *12 oz. can whole kernel corn*

- Preheat oven to 400 degrees.

- Grease skillet or pan and place in oven while preparing the ingredients. Place butter in a bowl and allow to soften at room temperature for 1 hour. Cream butter and add sugar and cream until semi-smooth. Combine flour, baking powder and cornmeal. Add to butter mixture and mix well. Add eggs and milk, beat until well blended. Add cheese and corn, beat 1 minute more. Pour into a 9-by-13-inch pan or skillet. Bake 25 minutes.

(Serves 8-10)

(NOTE: Bread will appear bubbly because of the Monterey Jack cheese. Nevertheless it will be done.)

ICE BREAKER CORNBREAD À LA ALBERT COLLINS

Master guitarist and blues legend Albert Collins named his band The Icebreakers, and they lived up to their name. No matter how cold the audience, Albert and his group would have them sizzling and cooking by the second song. I knew Albert but I don't have any idea whether he liked cornbread or not. No matter: I named this one after him because it has the same effect on diners as he had on audiences. Let a son-of-a-bitch walk into my kitchen and say, "I don't want nothing to eat and I'm really not into cornbread"... I'll give him/her a sliver right out of the oven and they'll respond, "damn, I stopped eating cornbread because nobody made it like my mother... but this is different."

- *1 cup yellow cornmeal*
- *1 cup flour*
- *3 tbsp. sugar*
- *1 tbsp. baking powder*
- *1 cup milk (room temperature)*
- *⅓ cup soft shortening (butter or bacon fat)*
- *2 eggs*

- Preheat oven to 400 degrees.

- Lightly grease baking pan or skillet and heat in oven while paring the above ingredients.

- Combine cornmeal, flour, sugar, and baking powder in a bowl and mix well. Add shortening and stir until well blended. Beat eggs and milk together and mix with dry ingredients until blended. Pour batter in a hot, well-greased skillet or 8-inch pan and bake in oven for 25 minutes or until done.

- Serve hot.

(Serves 6)

Contact (818) 366-0510/0520 fax
rawspltt@aol.com

Swamp Dogg

RAP BISCUITS DELIGHT

Very appropriately named because I've yet to see someone bite into one and be able to keep quiet. One of these, filled with butter, margarine, or whatever, will transform you into Snoop Dogg, LL Cool J, and Queen Latifah... You'll be talking shit all night.

- *2 cups all-purpose flour*
- *1 tbsp. lard or Crisco-type shortening (I prefer lard)*
- *Note: no salt*
- *1 tsp. baking powder*
- *¾ cup cold water*

- Preheat oven to 400 degrees.

- Mix flour and shortening together until well blended. Pour in cold water and mix into a large ball. Roll dough on a floured surface and cut out biscuits. Place on an ungreased baking sheet and bake for 20 minutes or until brown.

(Makes 8-10 biscuits)

"Soul Explosion 69"

Don't Miss The "BIGGEST SHOW of the YEAR,"
With The Soulful Sound Of,

JERRY WILLIAMS Doing "It's Still Good"

CANDACE LOVE — "Un Un Boy Thats A No No"

The BAR KAYS — "Soul Finger" — "A . J. The House Fly"

K. C.'S Own The FABULOUS RAYON'S

GENE KENNEYBREW & The SOUL SENSATIONS

September 19, 1969 -- 9 til 1 A.M.

M.C. — Dynamic DELL RICE

The Real Thing — CRIS KING

National Guard Armory

18th and Ridge — Kansas City, Kansas

TICKETS ON SALE:

FOSTER RECORD SHOP — Kanas City, Missouri
OKLAHOMA RECORD SHOP — Kansas City, Missouri

Tickets On Sale In Kansas City, Kansas

THE HUB BOOK STORE — 5th and QUINDARO
WOODIE'S RECORD SHOP — 27th and Brown
THE V. I. P. CLUB — 1934 North 5th Street

NOODLES NOODLES NOODLES NOODLES NOODLES NOODLES

TOMMY HUNT "HUMAN" NOODLES

"Oh Lord, why did you make me human"... this is the first line to Tommy's 1961 top-five smash "Human."

This man had an illustrious career starting in the '50s with the Flamingos and sharing lead vocal chores with Nate Nelson. Singing his natural ass off was not enough for Tommy. He was extremely handsome... almost pretty, and every time he walked on stage, the ladies would yell and cry to the extent that through most of his performances, he seemed to be pantomiming... you couldn't hear shit!

When I started work for Musicor records in '67, Tommy was assigned to me to produce. We hit it off immediately and still remain friends. He resides in Amsterdam, Holland, and is still knocking 'em dead.

I've had a hell of a lot of good times with Tommy... he's another artist I'd love to record again.

- *2 tbsp. onion powder*
- *4 oz. butter*
- *½ lb. thin spaghetti*
- *1 tbsp. parmesan cheese*

- Cook spaghetti according to instructions on the package, but rinse and drain in cold water. Set noodles in the refrigerator for 30 minutes to chill. Melt butter in frying pan, add noodles and onion powder to hot butter. Stir fry over a medium heat for 8 minutes.

- Top with parmesan and serve.

(Serves 4)

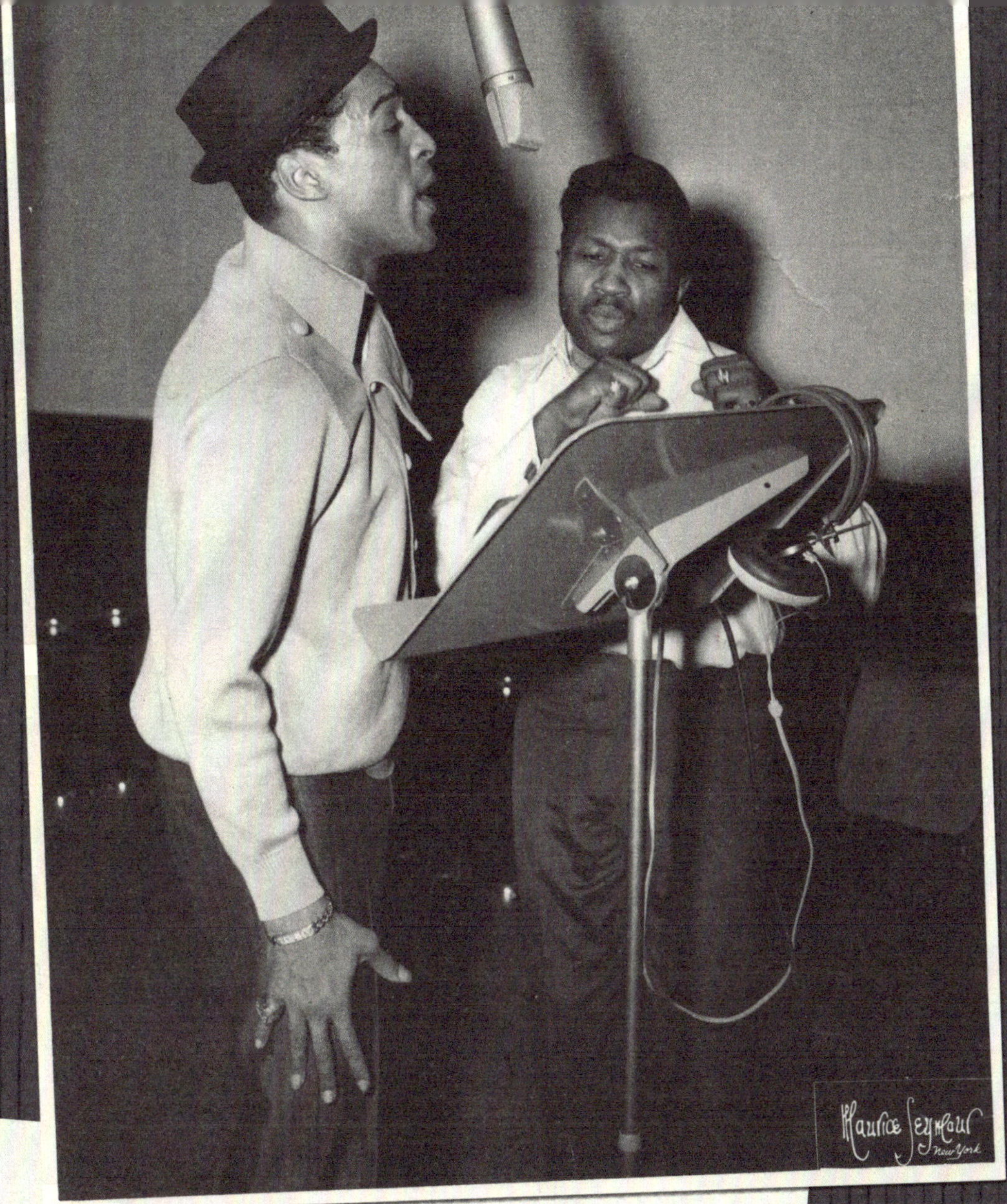

Tommy Hunt and me in Musicor studio ('68) overdubbing vocals on "Just A Little Taste," "Your Man," and "One-Two-Three." Tommy had anxiety attacks before doctors knew what they were. A singing motherfucker!

MIDEM'82
JERRY WILLIAMS
BBJ INT'L LTD.
UNITED KINGDOM

YOCK A MEIN 78 RPM

I thought this was a Chinese dish until I ventured outside of Virginia and tried to order it... everybody responded as though I was a little touched in the cranium. Every Chinese restaurant in Virginia has this on the menu.

Yock A Mein was so popular when I was a boy, that my family, neighbors, church, etc. would make Yock on the weekends and sell it to raise money for whatever was needed.

Later I found out that Yock A Mein was a dish created by the slaves and adapted by the Chinese who settled in Virginia.

Since the invention of records, we've gone through various revolutions per minute (RPMs) like 78 RPM, 16¾ RPM, 33⅓ RPM, and 45 RPM. This recipe's title pays homage to the RPMs I grew up on.

When you go to Virginia (Tidewater especially...) get some Yock A Mein.

- *⅓ cup sesame oil*
- *2 quarts of water*
- *5 to 6 pieces of chicken chopped*
- *I lb. of Yock A Mein noodles... (carry your ass to Chinatown)*
- *½ tsp. pepper*
- *1 cup flour*
- *8 tsp. finely chopped onion*
- *½ tsp. vinegar*
- *½ tsp. chili powder*
- *dash of cayenne pepper*
- *1 tbsp. of soy sauce*
- *3 tbsp. of ketchup*

- Put water in a Dutch oven, put the oil in a fry pan, and heat both. Put pepper and flour in a bag, add chicken, shake, and place in oil and cook over a medium flame till done (about 20 minutes), turning periodically to ensure browning on all sides. Bring water to a boil and gradually add spaghetti. Boil 10 minutes until tender, stirring frequently. When done, rinse with hot water. Chop onion very fine and put aside. Cool chicken and remove meat and skin from bone. Dice very small and set aside. Fill a soup bowl with noodles, add vinegar, cayenne pepper, soy sauce, ketchup, onions, chili powder, and 2 tbsp. of chopped chicken.

- Mix well with a large spoon and fork and serve.

(Serves 8)

FETTUCINI JERRY LEE LEWIS

I learned to play piano almost like Jerry Lee Lewis because I thought he was the coolest person in the world, and he was until he married Myra Brown, his thirteen year old cousin. Nevertheless, I named this recipe in his honor because his music has been instrumental in some of my successes and his personal life is still just that, his personal life.

- *1 lb. flat-shaped Italian fettucini*
- *1 tsp. olive oil*
- *2 cups melted butter*
- *¾ cup heavy cream*
- *¼ tsp. parsley flakes*
- *2 cups grated parmesan cheese*
- *fresh ground pepper*

- Cook the noodles in a large pot of boiling water, add the 1 tsp. of olive oil to the water, cook until tender. Drain very well in a colander. Place noodles in a warm casserole over low heat, add butter, parsley flakes, cream, and cheese. Toss concoction with tenderness and love until noodles are well saturated. Serve immediately with ground pepper to suit individual tastes.

- I can't emphasize the importance too much about serving this dish immediately because it gets cold very, very quickly.

(Serves 6-8)

EVERGREEN BALLROOM

OLYMPIA, WASHINGTON

MON. JULY 28th

SHOW AND DANCE - From 9 to 1 a.m.

"Whole Lot of Shaking Going On"

"Great Balls of Fire"

"Mean Woman Blues"

"High School Comfidential"

"Breathless"

JERRY LEE LEWIS

TILGHMAN PRESS - 1201 - 32N

NY

SPAGHETTI AND MEATBALLS LL COOL J

LL is the first rapper whose work I could really appreciate and identify with. He remains one of the world's best rappers and writers today. In his honor, I've named one of my best dishes after him.

I can't say I know him... though my friend and the second biggest Swamp Dogg fan in the world Bernard Byer, installed the cable in the house of Charlie Fisher, who's LL's manager and shook Bernard's hand. So we're damn near family?

TRACK I (MEATBALLS)

- *2½ lbs. ground beef*
- *3 eggs beaten*
- *2 tbsp. parsley flakes*
- *½ tsp. garlic powder*
- *½ cup unflavored bread crumbs*
- *1 tsp. black pepper*

- With a spoon or hand mix all ingredients together and make into balls. (approximately 20). Place in fry pan over low heat, cover, and brown on all sides. Save drippings for Track II (sauce).

------>

See next page for Track II & III

TRACK II (SAUCE)

- *8 Italian sweet sausages*
- *8 Italian hot sausages*

- Cover with water in a fry pan and cook over medium heat until water boils out.

  - *3 tbsp. olive oil*
  - *1 green pepper diced*
  - *3 small onions diced*
  - *1 long celery stalk diced*

- Put drippings and oil from Track I in a fry pan, sauté green pepper, onions, and celery until tender.

- ADD:

  - *2 tbsp. parsley flakes*
  - *2 tbsp. basil leaves*
  - *1 tsp. sage*
  - *1½ tbsp. oregano*
  - *½ tsp. crushed red pepper*
  - *½ tsp. thyme*
  - *1 tbsp. minced garlic*
  - *¼ tsp. rosemary leaves*
  - *½ tsp. chili powder*
  - *1 tbsp. marjoram*
  - *1 tsp. tarragon leaves*

- Stir two minutes.

- ADD:

  - *2 29 oz. cans of tomato puree*

- Stir, cover, and cook over low flame for 1½ hours.

- Cut sausage into quarters and add to sauce. After ½ hour add 1 tsp. of sugar and the meatballs to the sauce, continue to cook for 15 minutes more. Let mixture stand.

TRACK III (SPAGHETTI)

- Cook spaghetti according to package directions but add 1 tsp. oregano and 1 tsp. of sage to water. Drain and place on platter and spread with sauce and meatballs.

(Serves 8-10)

Yvonne and me sitting on a fence in London immediately following hemorrhoid surgery and an anxiety attack.

The hemorrhoid specialist had me come to his office for the ordeal, and before he operated (?) he said, "I have a son who is a doctor in Boston and he frowns on my hemorrhoid removal methods"... after he did it I was in total agreement with his son. This motherfucker was a maniac!

I dropped my pants, lay on my stomach. He parted my cheeks and wrapped rubber bands around each hemorrhoid and popped it in the same fashion as one would shoot a staple across the elementary school classroom. Immediately following I had to wear Kotex over my ass because I was bleeding like I had misscarriaged with an accompanying soreness that still takes precedence over any pain I've experienced in my entire life; this went on for two weeks. At night I slept with the sanitary pad and a torn sheet made into a a diaper to fit a hundred-and-ninety-pound baby.

La Belle Cuisine

When hair was essential... circa '74
1650 BROADWAY, SUITE 1211, NEW YORK, N.Y. 10019
TEL: 757-6921
JERRY WILLIAMS, JR.
A & R Director
LONSTAN PRODUCTIONS Inc.

FISH
FISH
FISH

LOUIS JORDAN SATURDAY NITE FISH FRY (SALMON CAKES)

September 9th, 1949, Louis Jordan had the number one record in America, "Saturday Night Fish Fry"-and that wasn't his only hit record that wore an epicurean name. He also did "Cole Slaw," "Beans and Cornbread," "Lemonade," "Hungry Man," "Lollypop," "A Chicken Ain't Nothing but a Bird," "Onion," "Salt Pork West Virginia," "That Chick's Too Young to Fry," and "Swinging in a Coconut Tree." Even in a number of his songs with non-foods, e.g., in "Deacon Jones," there's a line that goes "who gets all the chicken breast and leaves the gizzards for the rest... Deacon Jones, yes, yes."

Louis Jordan influenced the hell out of me... The first record I ever purchased was "Run Joe" by Louis.

The first music videos, then called "soundies," were produced by Jordan and his manager Milt Gabler in the 1940s. After producing them they contracted theaters throughout the country to show them. Jordan proved what MTV and BET found out forty years or so later that music soundies (videos) were a great promotional device.

I love this fellow Cancerian (7-8-1908) and I'm thinking about dedicating my next cookbook entirely to him.

- *1 15½ oz. can salmon*
- *1 egg beaten*
- *1 small onion diced*
- *1 cup oil*
- *½ tsp. pepper*
- *½ green pepper diced*

- Put all ingredients, except oil, in a bowl and mix well. Shape mixture into balls. On a floured board or floured wax paper, roll balls until floured on all sides. Heat oil and fry till golden brown on all sides.

- Serve with a White Cream Sauce.*

(Serves 9-12)

<u>WHITE CREAM SAUCE*</u>

- *2 tbsp. butter*
- *2 tbsp. flour*
- *1 cup milk*
- *dash of salt and pepper*
- *1 egg yolk*

- In a heavy pan or double boiler melt 2 tbsp. of butter, stir in 2 tbsp. of flour. Blend these 2 ingredients well, then slowly stir in 1 cup of milk. Bring to a slow boil, while stirring constantly. Cook for 3 minutes more. Add a dash of salt and pepper.

- This must be served hot. Approximately 2 minutes before I serve the sauce I beat in egg yolk and stir it into the sauce. Try it, it makes for a richer taste.

- Makes 1 cup.

(Serves 10-15)

FILÉ GUMBO FATS DOMINO

Gumbo always reminds me of two immediate things: Fats Domino and New Orleans. In that order.

Filé is the kickass seasoning that separates this from being just a great seafood stew. How does Fats fit into this? He was the kickass ingredient that when added to New Orleans music made it a treat to musical palates all over the world. He also is one of my heaviest musical influences and can be found running intricately through one or more songs on every Swamp Dogg album I've ever recorded.

TRACK I

- *½ cup olive oil*
- *2 tbsp. butter*
- *3 onions diced*
- *1 tsp. minced garlic*
- *1 tbsp. fennel (chopped)*
- *1 tsp. saffron*
- *2 bay leaves*
- *2 tbsp. tomato paste*
- *¼ tsp. celery seed*
- *4 tbsp. parsley (chopped)*
- *1 tsp. pepper*

- In a large pot heat olive oil and butter. Add the ingredients and cook until transparent.

TRACK II

- *3 tbsp. Wondra*
- *8 chicken wings*
- *1 tsp. thyme*
- *1 tsp. red pepper*
- *water to cover*
- *32 oz. can tomato puree*
- *1 tbsp. lemon juice*
- *¼ cup dry white wine*

- Add Wondra to Track I and stir until you get a paste. Add all of the other ingredients in Track II with water to cover. Simmer 30 minutes.

------>
See next page for Track III

TRACK III

- *water (cover ingredients below)*
- *6 lobster tails cracked*
- *6 king crab legs*
- *2 lbs. filet flounder*
- *1 lb. shrimp*
- *1 lb. scallops*
- *64 oz. frozen okra*
- *Creole gumbo filé*

- Add lobster tails to Track II and cook ½ hour. Next add the king crab and cook 15 minutes. Next add the filet and okra and cook 15 minutes. Stir in shrimp and scallops and cook 8 minutes more. Remove from heat. Mix 6 tbsp. of the soup, with 4 tbsp. of gumbo filé. Put a teaspoon of filé mixture in each individual bowl. Never put it in the pot because it will become glue.

- Serve with French garlic bread.

(Serves 10-15)

My wife loves my cooking

Father & Daughter Dance with Jocelyn...
Afterwards she poisoned the band.
Just kidding! Only the guitar player.
SWAMP

GOSPEL BIRD & FAMILY GOSPEL BIRD & FAMILY GOSPEL BIRD & FAMILY GOSPEL BIRD & FAMILY

CHICKEN 'N' DUMPLINGS GUITAR SLIM

"The Things That I Used to Do." Now that was a hit, and most deservedly so.

The first of about ten times that I saw Guitar Slim, I was in more than awe; I was spiritually lifted and inspired. For clarification, I consider each time he came to town to appear as one of the twenty times, but I used to sit through at least two shows each day of his two-day appearances. Guitar Slim put the icing on the cake in relation to me confirming the fact that show business would be my life.

Yellow suit, green suit, pink suit... What kind of wonderful shit is this? Guitar Slim wore suits in every wild color imaginable, had his name on the body of his guitar and also in the right hand side of the back window of his brand new yellow 1954 Cadillac Coupe de Ville. He was tall, hair slicked to the brain, a big diamond ring, and a face that would have been Denzel Washington at that time. Ask me what I want to be... president, fireman, or Guitar Slim? Hands down, no contest, let me be Eddie Jones a.k.a Guitar Slim.

This soliloquy doesn't have anything to do with chicken 'n' dumplings but it doesn't have to-it's my cookbook.

- *3 quarts water*
- *¼ cup butter*
- *1 chicken cut up*
- *2 cups flour*
- *1 large yellow onion, quartered*
- *¼ tsp. pepper*
- *1 tsp. parsley flakes*

- Place butter and 2 cups of water in a sauce pan and heat until butter is melted, then place the "butter water" in the freezer until you are ready (approx. ¾ hour). Put chicken and the remaining water in a pot and cook covered over at low heat for 2 hours. Combine flour, onion, pepper, parsley flakes and add "butter water" one tablespoon at a time until dough can be made into a ball. Turn dough onto floured surface and roll very thin, cut into 2-inch strips. Turn flame higher under pot. Place strips in pot with chicken one at a time. Never place strips on top of each other because they will stick together. Nevertheless, placing them on top of each other at 2-minute intervals and stirring after each interval will avoid the sticking hazard. After the addition of the last strip, stir and remove pot from flame. Let cook 10 minutes uncovered. It's ready.

(Makes 6-8 servings)

EDWIN BIRDSONG, ME, DON COVAY, BROOK BENTON (NYC)... when shoes were important

DON COVAY, ME, HAROLD CARTER, BILL STATON, ,circa '72. . a Swamp birthday

DON COVAY SMOTHERED CHICKEN HAVE MERCY, HAVE MERCY BABY

When I lived in East Elmhurst and West Hempstead, N.Y., Don Covay and his wife Yvonne were among our best friends and they loved my smothered chicken. Don was a nut. Early on, he wasn't big; a crazy guy we just laughed at. But then he wrote hit after hit. He wrote ten top-five fucking records. "See-Saw," "Shingaling," "Chain of Fools," "Sookie Sookie," "Pony Time"-he used to say "Get up, it's pony time!" then make a sound like a pony. And of course, "Mercy Mercy," which I named this chicken after.

- *8 chicken legs or thighs or whatever*
- *2 tbsp. oil*
- *1½ cups of all-purpose flour*
- *3 tbsp. Wondra flour*
- *1 tsp. pepper*
- *3 tbsp. onion powder*
- *2½ cups water*

- Put chicken, onion powder, pepper, and flour in a bag and shake. Place coated chicken in hot oil and cover. Cook over medium heat till semi-crisp (10 minutes). Remove chicken to a bowl, drain all the oil, keeping 1 tablespoon. Sprinkle 3 tbsp. of Wondra in the oil and stir till brown. Add water gradually and slowly stir constantly to avoid lumps. Place chicken in skillet, baste, cover and simmer for 15 minutes more.

(Serves 4)

VIRGIN CHICKEN JOHN WOOLER

John is the V.P. of Virgin Record's Pointblank label, to which I happen to be signed. He's also a dear friend-how do you think I got signed? Just kidding... He signed me because he felt the same as my wife and manager: that I was reeking with talent, overflowing with new ideas, and cheap to record-a low-maintenance act.

I introduced John's taste buds to this recipe during our first dinner meeting at my house and he went over the epicurean edge, more so than anyone else who's ever orally partook of this effort. Therefore, it is without hesitation that I name this in his honor. Nevertheless, I still don't know why John aided and abetted in giving Michael Jackson's sister eighty-million dollars and won't validate my parking... Is he trying to tell me something?

- *1 fryer (cut up)*
- *1 cup oil*
- *1 large onion (cut into 4-6 wedges)*
- *⅔ cup flour*
- *4 tbsp. paprika*
- *3 tsp. pepper*
- *Worcestershire sauce*

- Heat oil in frying pan, reduce heat to medium and add onion wedges. Combine flour, paprika, and pepper in a paper bag. Shake the bag to distribute ingredients, then add chicken (couple pieces at a time). Shake chicken and add to oil. After all pieces have been added, continue to fry uncovered for 20 minutes or until delightfully brown, turning occasionally. Pad a basket/bowl with paper towels, put the chicken in, and douse generously with Worcestershire while hot.

(Serves 5-6)

Vera and Jerry. Mother & Father Family reunion... Long Island ('74)

Wally Roker..he eats, and eats, and eats, and eats, and eats, and eats,

and eats..

SWEET 'N' SOUR CHICKEN
WALLY ROKER

Wally Roker loves this recipe, and if you've seen his picture in this book you'll conclude that he loves everything else in this book too. Who's Wally? Only one of the greatest and most creative bass singers to emerge in the '50s. That's him you hear singing down in the basement with The Heartbeats on "A Thousand Miles Away," "Wedding Bells," "I Found A Job," "Down On My Knees," and many others. Wally also gave birth to the first Swamp Dogg album, *Total Destruction To Your Mind*, on his highly successful Canyon record label.

TRACK I

- *6 chicken thighs or small breasts (filet and cut into ½-inch cubes)*
- *½ tsp. sugar*
- *1 tbsp. soy sauce*
- *2 tbsp. cooking sherry*
- *½ tsp. pepper*

- Put sugar, soy sauce, sherry, and pepper in a small mixing bowl. Add chicken, saturate, and let marinate for ½ hour.

TRACK II

- *2 tbsp. oil*
- *1 can pineapple chunks*
- *2 carrots (peeled, cut into ¼-inch cubes) parboil in water for 7 minutes*
- *1 green pepper (cut into 1-inch pieces diagonally)*
- *2 tbsp. oil*
- *1 tsp. minced garlic*
- *1-inch piece of ginger root*

- Heat oil, add garlic and ginger root, stir fry 3 minutes. Add vegetables and stir fry over low flame for 10 minutes more. Set to the side.

TRACK III

- *1 egg*
- *2 tbsp. flour*
- *1 tbsp. water*

- Combine egg, flour, and water, making a smooth batter. Remove chicken from marinade and dip chicken into batter using fingers. Drop into hot oil and fry covered until crisp over a medium flame. Combine chicken with vegetable mixture.

------>
See next page for Track IV

- *½ cup sugar*
- *½ cup apple cider vinegar*
- *2 tbsp. soy sauce*
- *2 tbsp. cooking sherry*
- *3 tbsp. tomato ketchup*
- *2 tbsp. cornstarch*
- *½ cup pineapple juice (water can be substituted)*

- Place sugar, vinegar, soy sauce, sherry, and tomato ketchup in a sauce pan and bring to a boil. Pour sauce over chicken and vegetables. Combine cornstarch and pineapple juice stir till smooth. Place chicken, vegetables and sauce over a very low flame and add cornstarch mixture, stirring occasionally until sauce thickens.

- Serve over rice.

(Serves 4)

GUITAR

BLACK records TOP

GUITAR SHORTY

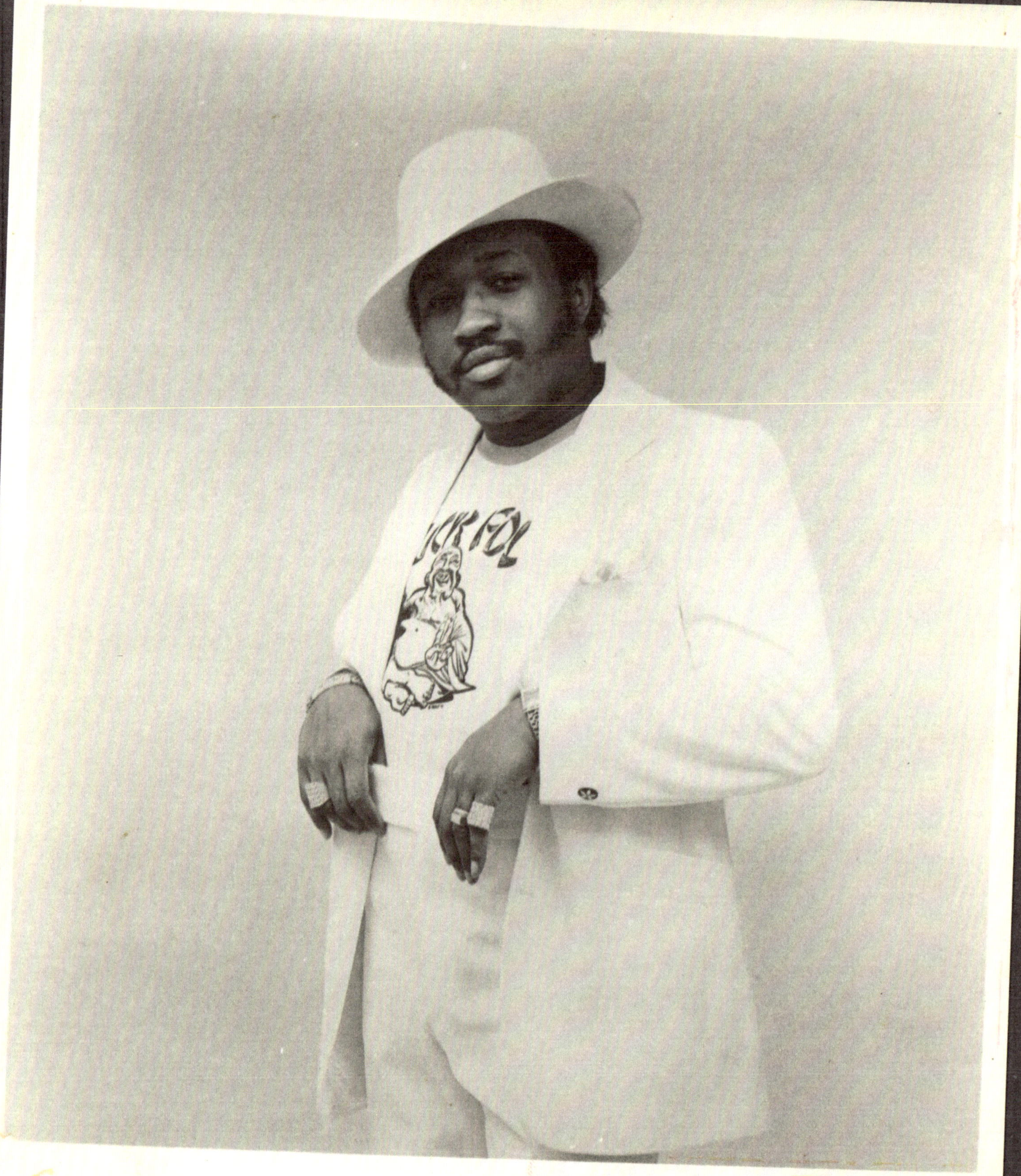

SWAMP DOGG

ATOMIC ART RECORDS
0402 Sunset Blvd. Suite 3E
Hollywood, Calif. 90069

SWAMP DOGG FRIED CHICKEN

- 4 pieces of chicken (parts of your choice)
- ⅓ cup oil
- ⅓ cup flour
- ½ tsp. pepper
- 2 tbsp. poultry seasoning
- 2 tsp. nutmeg

- Heat oil in frying pan. Put flour in a paper bag. Add pepper, poultry seasoning, and nutmeg to flour and shake bag to mix thoroughly. Add the chicken, shake well. Remove from bag and place in frying pan over medium heat. Cover and cook for 20 minutes or until brown on all sides, turning periodically to obtain even doneness.

(Serves 3-4)

HERB FRIED CHICKEN
FATS WALLER

Thomas "Fats" Waller had more personality than any ten entertainers you can name, past or present. Fats sold millions of records, charmed millions of moviegoers, and wrote a multitude of songs ("Ain't Misbehavin'," "I've Got a Feeling I'm Falling," "Valentine Stomp," "Your Feet's Too Big," "Yacht Club Swing," "Off-Time") that have endured the test of time. He was a big influence on my life, and on my facial expressions and stage presence. Thanks, Fats.

- *6 pieces chicken (thighs or breasts)*
- *3 tbsp. lemon juice*
- *¾ cup flour*
- *½ tsp. pepper*
- *1 tbsp. parsley flakes (dried)*
- *1 tsp. thyme leaves*
- *1 tsp. marjoram leaves*
- *2 tsp. rosemary*
- *1 tsp. basil*
- *½ tsp. paprika*
- *5 tbsp. shortening*
- *3 chicken bouillon cubes*
- *1 10oz. can cream of mushroom soup*

- Put lemon juice in a small mixing bowl, then dip chicken in lemon juice and place on a plate. Put flour, pepper, paprika, thyme, marjoram, basil, rosemary, and ½ of the parsley flakes into a bag. Shake to mix ingredients well. Put chicken into bag 2 pieces at a time and shake well. Place chicken on a rack, save remaining flour for gravy. In a skillet melt shortening. When hot add chicken and cook slowly until brown on all sides. After browning, place chicken in a 2-quart baking dish. Dissolve bouillon cubes in 3 cups boiling water, pour over chicken, then sprinkle chicken with remaining parsley and rosemary. Place chicken in a 375-degree oven uncovered for 55 minutes.

- Save 2 tbsp. of the shortening and all the pan dripping. Stir in 3 tbsp. of remaining flour (slowly). When flour is smooth add very slowly 2 cups milk stirring constantly. Add cream of mushroom soup. Continue to cook slowly until the gravy thickens. Pour over chicken.

(Serves 3-4)

Cameo Studio in Philadelphia, 1971... with Richard Rome and some symphony strings

HOT BUTTERED SOUL TURKEY

- *1 turkey (10 lbs.)*
- *2 sticks butter*
- *3 tbsp. poultry seasoning*
- *3 tbsp. sage*
- *1 tbsp. pepper*
- *2 quarts of water*
- *neck and giblets*
- *3 tbsp. Wondra (browned)*
- *1 tbsp. butter*

- Remove neck and giblets from turkey cavity. Place in 1½ quarts of water with 1 tbsp. each of poultry seasoning, onion powder, and sage. Boil over a low flame for ¾ of an hour. Remove from pot and set aside.

- Saturate turkey on all sides with poultry seasoning, then pat on sage and pepper. Place butter in cavity. Wrap turkey in aluminum foil (shiny side down), place on a rack back side down in a roasting pan with bottom covered completely with water. Cover roasting pan and bake in oven at 350 degrees for 1½ hours. Remove turkey from oven and gently open foil, baste turkey from cavity, restore aluminum foil, cover, and bake 1 more hour. Remove from oven and keep covered until time to slice and serve.

- In a skillet melt the 1 tbsp. of butter, stir in the flour, add the broth a little at a time until you reach your desired consistency. Chop the giblets and add to gravy with a dash of pepper. Stir and serve with turkey.

- The neck? Give it to the one who requests it... Bypass me.

(Serves 12-15)

BIG TURKEY THIGHS MAYBELLE

Big Maybelle was four-hundred pounds plus but that didn't hinder her from becoming a top-draw performer and consistent record seller. "Candy," her national anthem, "Don't Let The Sun Catch You Crying," "96 Tears," "Gabbin' Blues," "My Country Man," and "Do Not Pass Me By" were a few of the hit records by Maybelle Smith.

I am proud to be able to say that I knew this blues legend who always performed barefooted; this was her trademark and her comfort zone.

TRACK I

- *6 large turkey thighs (boned and skinned)*
- *1 tsp. pepper*
- *2½ cups water*

- Wash and pepper the thighs, place in a shallow pan with water, and bake at 300 degrees for 2½ hours.

TRACK II

- *½ cup enchilada sauce*
- *1 cup tomato paste*
- *1½ cups water*
- *½ lb. Monterey Jack cheese*
- *2 oz. Spanish olives (drained)*

- In a sauce pan combine enchilada sauce, tomato paste, olives, and water. Simmer over a low heat for 10 minutes. Tum off heat and stir in cheese.

TRACK III

- *8 oz. sour cream*
- *2 stalks chopped scallions*
- *2 cups cooked white rice*

- Combine sour cream and scallions. In a serving dish spread the rice, place turkey on rice, and spoon Track II over both.

- Spread sour cream and scallions over Track II and serve.

(Serves 6)

Stanley Vanleer Productions, Inc.
1650 Broadway - Suite 1211
New York City, N.Y. 10019
SVP inc.
Jerry Williams, Jr.
Tel: 757-5970

PHIL JONES
TURKEY SCALLOPINI

Phil was the vice president of the Fantasy record group which includes Stax, Specialty, Riverside, Prestige, Pablo, Contemporary, Milestone, Volt, Enterprise, Swingsville, and so on. Back in the '80s, they were buying up everything. Phil was also my buddy and the person who had enough nerve to sign me in '91 and unleashed my *Surfin' in Harlem* album on the public.

Phil has never eaten any of my cooking in my presence but he published excerpts from this cookbook which were used as a promotional companion to the *Surfin' in Harlem* album with this recipe among them.

Phil is the last of the people who really knows the record business... CD business... cassette business... whatever this is these days. What do you call it?

- *4 tbsp. oil*
- *4 tbsp. butter*
- *2 lbs. turkey breasts (sliced)*
- *¼ tsp. white pepper*
- *½ tsp. ground oregano*
- *1 tsp. marjoram leaves*
- *2 tbsp. parmesan cheese grated*
- *1 tsp. parsley flakes*
- *⅓ cup burgundy*
- *8 oz. tomato sauce*
- *4 oz. can sliced mushrooms*

- Heat oil and butter. Sprinkle turkey slices with parmesan and sauté on both sides. Add oregano, marjoram, parsley flakes, and mushrooms. Cook and stir fry for 7 minutes more. Add wine cover and cook for an additional 3 minutes. Add tomato sauce, cover, and simmer for 10 minutes. Serve over rice.

(Serves 6-8)

KING ERRISSON BAHAMA TURKEY

King Errisson, who's from the Bahamas and played drums for years for Neil Diamond, taught me how to cook this dish after my wife Yvonne and my daughter Jeri and I raved over it on several occasions while dining with him and his wife Katie... him and his wife Princess... him and his wife Carol... This dish is only equaled by the percussionism he's displayed over the past fifteen years on records and stage with his employer Neil.

Although he and I aren't speaking and possibly never will again because of some dumb shit, this recipe is too good to be surrendered to obscurity because of King's West Indian ego. Oh no, I'm definitely not at fault.

- *6 turkey wings*
- *1 clove garlic diced or 2 tsp. garlic powder*
- *½ tsp. oregano*
- *½ tsp. black pepper*
- *1⅓ cup soy sauce*
- *3 tsp. paprika*
- *2 tsp. ginger*
- *¼ cup sesame oil*
- *3 green peppers (strips)*
- *4 onions (quartered)*
- *5 large carrots sliced ¼ inch*
- *2 tsp. thyme*
- *½ tsp. garlic powder*
- *28 oz. tomato sauce*
- *4 cups water (broth)*

- Split wings with a cleaver and chop each wing part into thirds. Place in a large pot with pepper, garlic, and oregano, cover with water and bring to a boil, reduce heat and let simmer for 25 minutes (covered). Save broth. Remove wings from pot, place on a large platter, saturate with soy sauce, paprika, and ginger. Heat oil in a large fry pan, sauté carrots (stirring constantly) about 10 minutes. Add green peppers (continue to stir) and sauté 5 minutes more. Add onions and sauté for 2 minutes more. Sprinkle in thyme and garlic powder. Sauté wings until brown on all sides. Add vegetables and tomato sauce to 2 cups of broth, add wings, cover, and simmer over low flame for 30 minutes. Using some of the remaining broth, cook your favorite rice and make a bed for the turkey and vegetables.

- Serve the tomato sauce broth as an optional au jus.

(Serves 10-12 hungry gorillas easily)

WYNONIE DRUNKEN SWEET 'N' SOUR CHICKEN HARRIS

Wynonie "Mr. Blues" Harris... Here we are again... sitting in the Capitol Theatre watching a stage show billed as the "Battle of The Blues" starring Wynonie Harris and Larry Darnell, two of the prettiest and talented niggers in show business in those days and they were recording hits, selling records, and packing 'em in.

Wynonie was another influence on my blues delivery, which during the '50s and '60s was more of a style called "shouting the blues." He went gold with "Drinking Wine Spo-Dee-O-Dee," "Bloodshot Eyes," "Sittin' on It All the Time," "All She's Wants to Do Is Rock," and "I Like My Baby's Pudding," and he would grace the stage with his band and sing the dog shit out of these and lots more.

Wynonie was always a little tipsy because he loved his alcohol, and it seemed to make his hazel eyes just glassy enough to hypnotize the audience so he could have his way with them... Throwing his head from side to side and making his processed hair fly up and down, up and down to his infectious blues-groove-ridden orchestra.

Wynonie would appreciate this dish, especially the vodka portion.

TRACK I (INTRODUCTION: SWEET 'N' SOUR SAUCE)

- *1 cup sugar*
- *1 cup vinegar*
- *4 tbsp. soy sauce*
- *4 tbsp. cooking sherry*
- *4 tbsp. ketchup*
- *4 tbsp. cornstarch*
- *1 cup water*
- *½ cup 100-proof vodka*

- Put the sugar, vinegar, soy sauce, sherry, and ketchup in a sauce pan and bring to a slow boil. Remove from heat. Mix cornstarch and water together, place to one side.

- Drink the vodka... you are now ready for track II.

------>

See next page for Track II

- *2 lbs. boneless chicken breasts (cut in 1-inch strips)*
- *½ tsp. sugar*
- *2 tbsp. soy sauce*
- *¼ tsp. pepper*
- *2 onions (cut in quarters)*
- *2 green peppers (cut in 1-inch strips)*
- *6 slices canned pineapple (cut in 1-inch chunks)*
- *6 carrots (cut in 1-inch pieces)*
- *12 maraschino cherries*
- *2 eggs*
- *4 tbsp. flour*
- *2 tbsp. water*
- *6 tbsp. sesame oil*
- *1 thin slice ginger root*
- *1 clove garlic*
- *½ cup vodka*

- In a large bowl mix sugar, soy sauce, sherry, and pepper. Add the chicken, toss around until well coated, and let marinate for 30 minutes. Bring some water to boil and cook carrots for 5 minutes. Drain and rinse under cold water. Make a batter by combining the eggs, flour, and water. Put 2 tbsp. of sesame oil in a large fry pan, skillet, wok, whatever, and stir fry garlic and ginger. Remove garlic and add vegetables, stir fry approximately 5 minutes. Remove vegetables from the fry pan with a slotted spoon, place in a large pot and add the sweet 'n' sour sauce. Pour the 2 tbsp. of oil out of the pan and wipe clean. Heat the remaining 4 tbsp. of sesame oil for deep frying. Fry the chicken strips and add to the vegetables and sauce. Add cornstarch mixture and stir over a low flame until the entire mixture thickens.

- Drink the vodka.

- Serve over rice or whatever. After the second vodka you could give less than a damn. Your job is done.

(Serves 6-8)

Baker Jones, my grandfather... taught me how to shoot a gun, ride a bike and what my wee wee was for. He was the dominant male role model in my life... a good one!

Georgia Jones, my grandmother... She could really lay down some lasting ass whippings

Our houseboat in Muscle Shoals... Little Jeri was conceived here, Ruth Brown was cursed out here, I damn near died here after greedily eating three pounds of poke(?) salad over a weekend alone. I was not cognizant of the fact that this salad was used as a purgative. I almost shit my way into a coma and lost about ten pounds instantly. I haven't cooked any since.

The Cherokee Six. Swamp Dogg Airways... Muscle Shoals... 1974

Sam Watkins, my father-in-law, and Howard Roberts, one of Alabama's richest, at my Long Island home ('74). As a friendship offering Howard gave me a Cherokee Six aircraft. Now that's friendship for your ass.

JAMES BROWN IN FLIGHT

"...Mama come here quick and bring me that licking stick"... James Brown, nineteen sixty eight. Another hero of mine, James broke down lyrical musical and entrepreneurial doors, thus showing the world that a black semi-educated person can own a hotel chain, Lear jets, broadcasting stations, and have people lined up around Madison Square Garden to see him Mash Potato. Without a godfather dedication this book wouldn't be shit.

- *16 chicken wings (cut off little pointed arms)*
- *⅓ cup oil*
- *¾ cup chili powder*
- *5 tbsp. Worcestershire sauce*
- *¼ cup parmesan cheese*
- *½ cup paprika*
- *¼ cup garlic powder*
- *2 large onions sliced*
- *1 green pepper sliced*
- *1½ cups water*
- *1 cup ketchup*
- *⅛ tsp. cayenne pepper*

- Heat oil in a skillet. Combine chili powder, paprika, and garlic in a small container with a lid or a paper bag. Place chicken wings in mixture two at a time, shake quickly and put into hot oil. Sauté over medium heat in covered pan until semi-done on one side, then turn. Remove from pan, put onion and green pepper in remaining oil, and sauté. Add water, ketchup, cayenne pepper, and Worcestershire sauce to the pan and put chicken back into mixture, cover, and simmer for ½ hour.

- Sprinkle with parmesan cheese and serve over rice.

(Serves 4-5)

SWAMP DOGG CHICKEN LOGS

- *6 large chicken breasts (fileted and skinned)*
- *6 slices boiled ham*
- *6 slices Swiss cheese*
- *1 stick butter*
- *½ cup flour*
- *8 oz. can sliced mushrooms*
- *½ cup Chablis*
- *2 tablespoons of flour*
- *pepper to taste*

- Lay the breast out on a cutting board with the side that was skinned facing down. Pound gently with a meat mallet until the breast appears thin and wider. Sprinkle lightly with pepper. Place one ham slice on the breast followed by one cheese slice on the ham. Roll the breast, ham, and cheese into a tight log and secure it with two skewers forming an X, or if you're sensational, which I'm not, tie the breast log with some heavy white sewing thread.

- Melt the butter in a skillet over a very low heat so it won't burn and smoke. Put the ½ cup of flour in a bag, drop the breast in two at a time, shake, and place in skillet when it's hot enough to sauté at low heat. Brown the breast all around, remove from skillet, and place in a casserole dish. Add the 2 tablespoons of flour to the skillet drippings and stir with a wire whisk until brown and blended. Add 1 cup of hot water gradually to the flour and drippings, stirring constantly. Now add the wine and mushrooms, stir about 1 minute more, then pour the mixture over the breast, cover and place in a 350-degree oven for about 1 hour.

- Serve immediately.

(Serves 6 small appetites or 3 big appetites)

I LOVe YOU DADDY
WILLIAMS
I LOVe YOU
I LOVe YOU

SWAMP DOGG RIDES AGAIN—"A major step forward," is what Nashboro Records calls its new alliance with Jerry Williams, known professionally as Swamp Dogg, young producer for whom the company is creating a new label, "Mankind Records". Under terms of the agreement only Williams' productions will appear on the Mankind Label which joins the Nashboro Group of Excello, Nasco, Creed, Abet and Kenmore. Nashboro also handles national distribution for Audio Arts. Shown after signing of the agreement are (seated) Jerry Williams, (standing) Freddie North, national promo director of Nashboro and an artist on its Abet label, Bud Howell, president of Nashboro, Bob Tubert, president of Excellorec Music Co., the affiliated publishing company of Nashboro and Robert Fitzpatrick, attorney representing Jerry Williams.

PORK PORK PORK PORK

LIONEL (HAM)PTON

In 1961, I replaced Pinocchio James as the singer for Lionel's big band at Pinocchio's request, while he recuperated from the flu. Here I was, twenty years old, in Washington, D.C., for the opening of the WOOK TV station, standing beside Lionel's vibraphone and singing my black ass off. "Honey Hush," "Flip Flop and Fly," and "Since I Fell For You"... I'm shouting the blues and his band is performing a colectomy on me and I got paid. I would have paid him. A singer has not lived unless he or she has had the opportunity to stand in front of a Lionel Hampton or Duke Ellington or Count Basie or Woody Herman or their equivalent and belt their little hearts out.

- *1 6½ lb. smoked ham*
- *whole cloves to taste*
- *2 12oz. can Coca-Cola*
- *½ cup brown sugar*
- *½ tsp. dry mustard*
- *2 tbsp. orange juice*
- *1 scoop flour*

- Score ham in diamond patterns about ⅛-inch deep. Push cloves into each corner of the diamond. Place ham in a cooking bag with a scoop of flour. Pour the Coca-Cola over the ham, tie and then close cooking bag, place bag in a roasting pan, put pan in a 350-degree oven for 1 hour. Remove ham from oven, open bag and baste, put the ham back for another ½ hour. Take ham out again, mix together the brown sugar, dry mustard, and orange juice, spoon over the ham, tie bag back together, and put back in oven for ½ hour more.

(Serves 12-15 hearty appetites)

EASTMAN—SAFETY

The Great
AMERICAN
MUSIC HALL
SUN
SWAMP DOGG

SAM COOKE'D HAM FROM SMITHFIELD

If you don't prepare this ham correctly it will take your breath away with its saltiness. Naturally, I learned to prepare this from my family because it's not the kind of thing that comes naturally, not unlike Sam Cooke. How'd you like the way I slid that in from nowhere? Well, Sam was the first big star I had the pleasure of opening for, circa 1956 at either Midway Park or Sunset Lake Park in Chesapeake, Virginia. Sam was steps above nice, offered me encouragement, and watched my performances... totally unlike Chris Kenner ("I Like It Like That" and "Land of a Thousand Dances") who slapped the shit out of me when I descended from the outdoor stage and demanded that I be taken off the lineup for the second show. Sam, by contrast, applauded and smiled. I wasn't that fuckin' good to be a threat to Kenner; he had the number-one record in the country. I name this recipe for Sam and his goodness and wish we could still enjoy his "live" performances. As far as Chris Kenner is concerned, I wouldn't name a tumor after that big, black, ignorant, drunk, greasy, dead motherfucker!

- *Smithfield ham (10-12 lbs.)*
- *2 cups vinegar*
- *2 cups molasses*
- *whole cloves*
- *1 cup pickle juice*
- *1 cup brown sugar*

- Brush ham with a stiff brush to remove pepper (do not be alarmed if you see mold, it comes with the territory). Soak ham overnight (8 hours) covered with water, 1 cup vinegar, and 1 cup molasses. Remove ham and wash again. In a roasting pan, cover ham with water, remaining molasses, and vinegar and boil rapidly for 30 minutes. Cover the ham with newspaper and a cloth and let it set overnight in the same water. Discard newspaper/cloth, score and place cloves throughout each square. Combine brown sugar and pickle juice and cover the entire ham. Bake in a 325-degree oven for 3½ to 4 hours.

- Cool and slice.

(Makes 12-15 servings easily)

DANCING FEET... IF IT'S GREGORY HINES I DON'T MIND

- *8 large pig feet split in half but not detached*
- *6 quarts of water approximately*
- *2 large onions quartered*
- *4 cups brown vinegar*
- *2 tbsp. (level) crushed pepper*
- *2 bay leaves*
- *1 tbsp. minced garlic*
- *2 tbsp. parsley flakes*
- *2 lbs. canned sauerkraut*
- *2 carrots peeled and diced*
- *1 package frozen green beans*

- Wash and singe all hairs from pig feet. Put trotters, vinegar, red pepper, bay leaves, garlic, parsley flakes, onions, and carrots into water. Bring to a boil, then simmer uncovered for 3½ hours or until the meat starts to separate from the bone. Add sauerkraut and green beans and cook another ½ hour.

- Serve quickly and take yours first or you may be left holding your mouth over a frankfurter because this is goooo...od.

(Serves 6-8)

Swamp Dog's 'Stone' 45, Spurs Anti-Drug Drive

LOS ANGELES—"Sam Stone," a drug addiction ballad written by John Prine and recorded un- noticed by the composer several years ago, has surfaced by another artist as a good chart possibility and base for community action.

Renny Roker of Cream Records here reports that Swamp Dog's recording of the song, which deals with the plight of a Viet Nam veteran who returns with a heavy drug habit, has sold over 17,000 in Philadelphia. Swamp Dog re- cently worked a 38,000-attendance gospel show at the Robin Hood Dell there as special added attrac- tion because of the single's power there. Swamp Dog and Roker are set for two appearances on Target, a two-time-per-day show over WPVI-TV, Philadelphia.

Roker singled out WDAS-AM and FM, WFIL and WIBG as stations in Philadelphia which kicked off the record. Roker claims to have 75 stations cross country doing community features, based on the single, including such im- portant outlets as WVON, Chicago; KFRC, San Francisco; KRLA here; WWIN, Baltimore; WAOK, At- lanta and WRBD, Fort Lauderdale.

Spots Litigation

LOS ANGELES—Mount Wilson FM Broadcasters has filed suit in local Superior Court against Soul City One-Stop and Sam Bellis, claiming the one-stop hasn't paid $9,000 for a series of radio com- mercial airings.

SEPTEMBER, 9, 1972, BILLBOARD

sock it to 'em judge

the hip judge

PIGMEAT MARKHAM

PIGMEAT (SPARERIBS) MARKHAM

Take a seat... we're back at the Capitol Theatre and the comedian's comedian is on stage with his troupe enacting his famous skits "Here Comes the Judge" and "Pig You Got a Dirty Woman." Pigmeat rocketed to crossover fame after his performance of "Here Comes The Judge" was seen and sanctioned by Ed Sullivan on his number one *Ed Sullivan* TV show. Shortly after his appearance, Chess Records released the album and single which reached the number-four position on the national charts.

I waited for Pig after one of his shows and introduced myself as he was leaving the theater as an aspiring singer and fan. Apparently the Capitol had no back doors, or they were bolted at all times, because all loading and unloading was done through the front. Anyway, thank you Pig. This is my way to help immortalize your name and keep interest stirred.

- *2 medium-size slabs of pork ribs*
- *½ cup soy sauce*
- *1 cup orange marmalade*
- *1 tsp. garlic powder*
- *½ tsp. ground ginger*
- *dash of pepper*
- *¼ cup ketchup*
- *¾ cup water*
- *1 tsp. dried parsley flakes*
- *1 4 oz. can sliced mushrooms (drained)*

- Cut ribs in serving sizes and place in a roasting pan with the meaty side down and roast for 30 minutes at 450 degrees. Turn ribs over and continue to roast for 40 minutes more at 450 degrees. In a bowl mix together thoroughly soy sauce, marmalade, garlic powder, ginger, pepper, ketchup, water, parsley flakes, and mushrooms. Drain grease from pan then cover with mixture and bake ½ hour more, basting occasionally.

(Serves 6)

PORK CHOPS STUFFED WITH (CHARLEY) PRIDE

I met Charley Pride and had the pleasure of conversing with him in '72 at the Country Music Awards in Nashville. Gary Bonds and I were there because we had stumbled up on another hit... this time, country gold for "She's All I Got" by Johnny Paycheck, which by the way knocked Charley's "Kiss An Angel Good Mornin'" out of the number-one Billboard slot. He wasn't mad... why should he have been? He had been in the number-one position on at least ten occasions and went on to do it at least ten more.

Charley Pride is the only black person in the history of country music to reach stardom, and in his case, super stardom. Adored by rednecks, WASPs, Ku Klux Klan, Republicans, Democrats, independents, separatists, and a Volkswagen bus full of African Americans... most of us were unaware of him twenty years ago and some of us are still ignorant of his powerful presence and position.

If a Klansman can give him a standing ovation, a skinhead can buy his CD, and a racist can display his autographed photo, well then...

- *4 tbsp. bacon fat*
- *2 cups apples diced (unpeeled)*
- *2 tsp. sugar*
- *½ tsp. nutmeg*
- *¼ tsp. cinnamon*
- *4 pork chops (2-inch thick)*
- *1 egg*
- *2 tbsp. oil*
- *1½ cups breadcrumbs*

- In a saucepan put the bacon fat, apples, and sugar, cook for 5 minutes. Now add ½ cup breadcrumbs, nutmeg, and cinnamon. Split the pork chops to the bone and stuff with the above mixture. Sprinkle the remaining bread crumbs on some wax paper. Beat the egg and add the oil. Coat the pork chops with bread crumbs, then dip them into the egg mixture making sure the entire chop is covered. Now roll the chops on another piece of wax paper and place on a rack in a shallow roasting pan and roast uncovered at 325 degrees for 1½ hours.

(Serves 6)

POTATOES & YAMS POTATOES & YAMS POTATOES & YAMS

WILLIE NELSON POTATO PLATTER

I think Willie is the best who ever did it... and he's still getting away with it. I was a Willie fan when he was wearing short hair, tight suits, and ties. I can always listen to him sing "Georgia on My Mind" and duet with Julio Iglesias. Here's to Willie, and all the food I've eaten while I do.

- *4 large white potatoes*
- *1 cup milk*
- *1 cup water*
- *¼ cup canola*
- *1 10 oz. can condensed cream of mushroom soup*
- *1 onion*
- *¼ tsp. pepper*
- *½ tsp. paprika*

- Heat oil in frying pan. Peel potatoes and cut in ¼-inch slices. Put potato slices in hot oil and season with pepper, cover and fry for 10 minutes over a medium heat. Peel onion and slice into ¼-inch rings, pull rings apart, turn potatoes, and add onion. Cover and simmer for 15 minutes, turning often to ensure even cooking. Add soup, water, milk, and paprika and stir gently. Cover and simmer for 30 minutes. Stirring often so mixture won't stick.

- Great with steak, fried chicken, fried or baked pork chops, and ham.

- Serve hot.

(Serves 6)

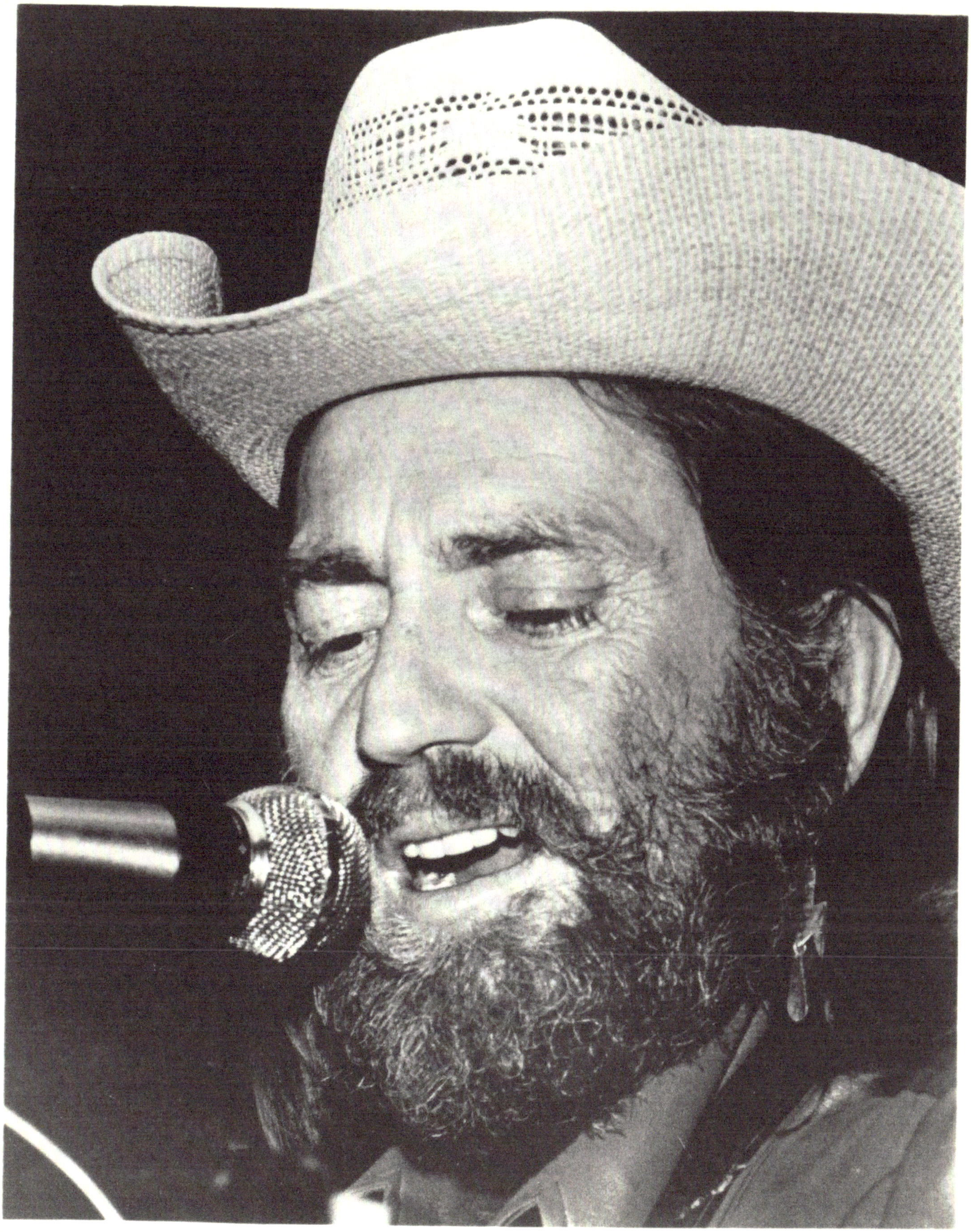

Representation:
Neil C. Reshen
New York, N.Y.

WILLIE NELSON

ATLANTIC RECORDS

GEORGE JONES POTATO PLATTER

George Jones is one of a kind. He earned the nickname "No-Show Jones" by not showing up for performances, and his fans always forgive him and buy tickets for his next scheduled appearance. George has gotten drunk and driven his car into trees, embankments, you name it, totaling his auto but walking away, every time, unscathed. George has admitted to consuming enough alcohol to kill all of Hell's Angels and I don't think he has an ulcer. George is unstoppable, immortal, and the greatest country artist in the world. His records have sold in the tens of millions and I defy anybody to open their minds and listen to some music by the Jones boy and not be captivated by his soul and sincerity.

I met George when he was recording for Musicor in the '60s and that was a memorable event for me.

George, this is my thank you for all of the wonderful music you've made for me to enjoy. Who's gonna fill your shoes?

- *4 large white potatoes*
- *1 cup milk*
- *1 cup water*
- *¼ cup canola oil*
- *1 10 oz. can condensed cream of celery soup*
- *1 onion*
- *2 tbsp. brandy*
- *¼ tsp. pepper*
- *½ tsp. paprika*

- Heat oil in frying pan. Peel potatoes and cut into ¼-inch slices. Put potato slices in hot oil, add pepper, cover and fry for 10 minutes over medium heat. Peel onion and slice into ¼-inch rings and pull apart. Turn potatoes and add onion and brandy, cover, and simmer for 15 minutes, turning often to ensure even cooking. Add soup, water, milk, and paprika and stir gently. Cover and simmer for 30 minutes, stirring often so mixture doesn't stick.

- Great with turkey, baked or fried chicken.

- Serve hot.

(Serves 6)

TRAFFIC JAM POTATOES
JAMES TAYLOR

Father's Day 1994, my family treated me to a James Taylor concert. I have about six albums by "Sweet Baby James" that I think contain some of the greatest performances and music ever captured on a record, and the other twelve albums I own aren't bad either.

Whenever I'm in a funk, I pull out some J.T. and let him sing the cobwebs from my mind.

Thank you James for always being where I can put my hands on you when I need you. I still see fire and I still see rain.

- *4 large white potatoes*
- *1 cup milk*
- *1 cup water*
- *¼ cup oil*
- *1 10 oz. can condensed cream of tomato soup*
- *1 onion*
- *½ green pepper diced*
- *¼ tsp. pepper*
- *½ tsp. paprika*

- Heat oil in frying pan. Peel potatoes and cut in ¼-inch slices. Put potato slices in hot oil. Add pepper, cover and fry for 10 minutes over medium heat. Peel onions and slice into ¼-inch rings. Pull rings apart, turn potatoes, and add green pepper and onions. Cover and simmer for 15 minutes, turning often to ensure even cooking. Add soup, water, milk, and paprika and stir gently. Cover and simmer for 30 minutes, stirring often so mixture doesn't stick.

- Great with barbecue, fried chicken, and pork chops.

- Serve hot.

(Serves 6)

ATTENTION DEE-JAYS!

OTIS REDDING

OTIS REDDING

LATEST SMASH ON VOLT RECORDS

BILLY YOUNG

OTIS REDDING'S BIG O PRODUCTIONS
present

BILLY YOUNG
"SAME THING ALL OVER"
JOTIS RECORDS

ARTHUR CONLEY
"I'M A STRANGER"
JOTIS RECORDS

ALL ARTISTS MANAGED EXCLUSIVELY BY
PHIL WALDEN ARTISTS & PROMOTIONS
PROFESSIONAL BUILDING--MACON, GEORGIA

GLOBE POSTER - BALTIMORE

POTATOES OTIS REDDING

1966... I'm on the road playing dives, blood buckets, and an occasional decent dump because of "Baby You're My Everything," one of my better records as Little Jerry Williams. I stop off in Macon, Georgia, to talk to Otis Redding. He says he wants me signing to his Redwald Booking Agency and opening for him. I'm happy as a pig in shit. Open for Otis? That's like having God's home number. Otis had told me that when I came to town, he'd take care of all my expenses. But there was a fuck-up... me. I didn't tell him when I was coming.

So I stroll into town, check into the Holiday Inn with my guitar player Billy Davis, a guy named Prince-who opened for me with his electric chair act which sucked-and his girlfriend-who Billy is banging the shit out of-so we are traveling with major tension. After running up a horrendous two-hundred-dollar hotel bill, I get a call from Otis telling me that he's leaving the next morning for Montreux and will get with me when he returns. Oh shit. I don't have any money so I attempt to skip out of the hotel. The result of this is incarceration in the Cook County jail... until Billy drives to Atlanta and gets an advance from B.B. Beamon, the promoter of my next gig, to satisfy the fine and Holiday Inn. The two days I am in jail, they serve pineapple sandwiches... have you ever heard of any shit like that?

But I'm still the luckiest guy in the world. I can fall in a pool of shit and come out smelling like a rose. Case in point: after my performances in Georgia, the Hifi Country Club in Charlotte, North Carolina, was next on the agenda. The night we arrived in Charlotte, Billy and I were beaten and thrown in jail for "robbing and assaulting" an elderly white couple who picked us out of a lineup. In Charlotte, we got two days of ass-kickings in jail... until we got let out because the cops realized that when the crime was perpetrated, I was in jail in Georgia. How do you like that for good luck?

Otis, I love you. And when I get to Heaven, although I really don't want to die, maybe we can finish our business.

- *4 large white potatoes*
- *1½ cups water*
- *¼ cup canola oil*
- *4 scallions*
- *¼ tsp. pepper*
- *1 tsp. parsley flakes*

- Heat oil in frying pan. Peel potatoes and cut into ¼-inch slices. Put potato slices in hot oil, add pepper, cover, and fry for 10 minutes over medium flame. Chop scallions, turn potatoes and add scallions and parsley flakes. Cover pan and simmer for 15 minutes, turning often to ensure even cooking. Remove top and add water. Simmer covered until water has been absorbed, stirring often, so the potatoes don't stick.

(Serves 6)

LARRY WILLIAMS POTATO BALLS

Potato balls are an apropos dedication to Larry Williams because he had big ones. Balls, that is. Pick up one of his albums and you'll see him pouring vintage champagne into the radiator of his Rolls Royce while wearing a full length mink coat and hat to match. And this was his shy side.

What little flamboyancy that I've employed in my off-and-on stage life was born from my first sight of Larry Williams. It was in Midway Park, Chesapeake, Virginia, nineteen fifty seven. The beach was jam-packed, Larry Williams was over an hour late, the crowd was restless, and the house band was just so-so. Then all of a sudden an amplified voice engulfed the crowd: "Everybody please move back from the stage," it said, "it's star time." While niggers were busy pushing and scrambling to adhere to this request, a brand new white Lincoln Continental convertible with the top dropped pulled up to the side of the stage.

The car came to a halt, Larry Williams put one foot on the top of the seat, leaped to the stage, did a spin, and stopped in front of the piano. The announcer bellowed, "Ladies and gentlemen... Larry Williams!" Like Cinderella, the "so-so" band was transformed into a rhythm and blues machine of musical poetry as they kicked off "Bony Moronie" and Larry commenced to sing, play, dance, and smile for an hour and a half. He did "Short Fat Fannie," "High School Dance," and a dozen more, for a dancing, screaming, loving crowd that would have died and gone to hell for him that night.

Larry died in 1980 from what was reported as a self-inflicted gunshot wound. The bullet was fired using his right hand although he was left-handed or vice versa. We can't get the answer on JFK, so we shouldn't ever expect to know the truth regarding Larry's demise, but we do know this... he was one of the baddest motherfuckers to ever emerge and help shape American rock 'n' roll.

- *6 quarts water*
- *5 pounds white potatoes peeled and sliced thin*
- *8 oz. of butter*
- *1 cup flour*
- *1 pound of thin sliced bacon*

- Preheat oven to 450 degrees.

- Bring water to a boil, add potatoes. Cook ½ hour uncovered. Drain in colander. Add the 8 oz. of butter and mash. Sit the mashed potatoes in the refrigerator until cool, about 45 minutes. After cooling, spoon out and shape potatoes in to balls (size? your preference, just don't be ridiculous). Roll balls lightly in flour, then wrap each ball with 2 slices of bacon crossing each other. Put balls in baking dish and place in oven and bake until bacon is cooked, approximately 45 minutes.

(Serves 15)

KORG
KORG
Politically Incorrect
Bill Maher
VILLAGE MUSIC
SWAMP DOGG
DON & DEWEY

ME, LUTHER DIXON, GARY BONDS..4/7/68
the opening of luther's Fox Den (Miami)

To "Jerry"
You've got to be the
best ever did it,
(what ever you're doing!)
Anyway, "You're still my
buddy
Gary U.S. Bonds

GARY U.S. BONDS

PREMIER TALENT ASSOCIATES, INC. 200 WEST 57TH STREET New York, N.Y. 10019 · 757-4300

YAMS GARY U.S. BONDS

We were a pair... together we did it all, at least once.

For the three of you who are brain-dead to Gary... he became a phenomenon in 1960 when he busted onto the music scene with what was to be known as the Norfolk sound, which consisted of an overpowering drum (mostly tom tom and bass), a bluesy alto sax played by Gene Barge a.k.a Daddy G, a bunch of homies screaming and clapping hands and Gary sing-screaming at the top of his lungs. All of these ingredients plus a guitar and bass were crammed onto one track (later two) that gave you a feeling when you listened that everyone was trying to escape off the record, which translated into some of the most danceable African-like records ever made... that's why he sold millions. "New Orleans," "Quarter to Three," "School Is Out," "Dear Lady Twist," and about ten more, with his last biggie being the Bruce Springsteen-produced "This Little Girl of Mine" in 1981.

I have some great memories of our life and times together, like the time we were in New York (circa 1968), bumped into Little Milton, and gave him the keys to a brand new Lincoln Continental and a suite at the Waldorf Astoria. What we forgot to tell Milton was that Hertz in Miami had a pickup out on the car and we had been kicked out of the Waldorf suite. In spite of these factors, he slept and drove for the three days he was there without a hitch. Then there was the time we were in Vegas together while he was appearing on the Dick Clark show and he almost drove Chuck Berry insane by distracting his daughter who he was trying to turn into the next Etta James(?). Chuck must have checked in and out of four hotels in an attempt to lose Gary. Then there was that other time that we bought hundreds of thousands of pesos from our friend(?) Troy Davis, only to discover that we had paid for a Cadillac but did not have enough pesos to fill it with gas, we lost a lot in the conversion. Following that came yet another time when Troy sold Gary a full-length mink coat for three hundred dollars and as always, had to have the money in advance, which we conceded to. Now comes the real shit... the coat is in Washington, D.C., but that's alright because Gary's getting his coat and I'm getting one the next day. So we jump in my newly leased Cadillac, head toward the Harlem tunnel, and hit the Pennsylvania turnpike... mink or bust! As we're driving through Delaware, Troy announces that we have to stop in Baltimore first because he has to buy his father a coat in order to get the mink coat that his father is holding hostage for an outstanding debt. We concede again. Once we reached Baltimore, Gary had to spend one hundred dollars to purchase Troy's father a coat. Four hundred dollars spent and we're headed to D.C. "Hello Mr. Davis"... that's when we discovered that our longtime friend was named Robert Madden. "How you doing Mr. Madden?" "Boy, where is my money?" "Come on, Dad, I bought you a coat, how you like it?" "That's fine, but what about my money you promised you were going to send right back to me?" "I had some problems, Dad... look here, Jerry, you and Gary let me have two hundred dollars for my ol' man, I'll straighten you when we get back to New York."

We conceded. Gary's got on his mink coat and boy it's worth all the trouble plus the six hundred and fifty dollars. Oh yeah! Troy didn't go back to New York with us because he had to close a big deal in D.C., the next day and needed another fifty... again we concede. We can deduct it from my coat. Mid-January, we drove back to New York with the top down on the car displaying the mink to the lowly travelers. All of a sudden it starts to rain as we exit the Harlem Tunnel and we got drenched pulling the top up because it stuck, but that's no problem for a mink coat.

When we pulled up to my house and walked inside drenching wet, Gary commenced to model the coat. Then Yvonne asked, "What's that smell"? "Smells like something died"... we're still admiring the coat. Then Yvonne ran her hands across the coat and said, "This is not mink, this is what's smelling"... "This is fun fur. You niggers have been taken by Troy again." As if that wasn't enough about a week later we were riding the subway and a passenger said to Gary, "Mister the fur is falling off your coat." When we confronted Troy his replies were "Well, the people told me it was mink" and "That was stupid of you to wear it in the rain." We ate some yams and said fuck it!

- *4 medium-sized uncooked yams*
- *¾ pound of marshmallows*
- *½ cup dark corn syrup*
- *1½ cups brown sugar*
- *1 tsp. ground nutmeg*
- *2 oz. stick butter*
- *1 orange*
- *1 lemon*

- Preheat oven to 350 degrees.

- Peel yams. Cut into ½-inch slices and place in a 6½-by-12-inch baking dish. Pour syrup evenly over yams . Sprinkle yams with brown sugar and nutmeg. Slice butter into ¼-inch pats and place randomly on top. Place dish covered in oven and bake for 45 minutes. Remove dish from oven and rearrange yams that the ones on top are on the bottom of the pan and vice versa. Slice the orange and lemon into ⅛-inch slices, keep rind intact and arrange on top of yams. Return dish to oven and bake covered for 25 minutes. Remove the dish from oven and cover the top with marshmallows. Bake uncovered for 15 minutes or until brown.

(Serves 8)

INVESTING IN (GARY) U. S. BONDS is Atco Records, as the label has signed the chanter to an exclusive disk pact. At the inking are (l. to r.) Atco execs Jerry Greenberg and Jerry Williams, and Gary U.S. Bonds. Several years ago, on the Legrand label, Bonds had a heavy hit with "Quarter To Three," and enjoyed success with such tunes as "New Orleans," "School Is Out," "Dear Lady Twist," and "Twist Twist Senora." The artist's first Atco single, "The Star," was released last week and is obtaining good airplay.

Billboard ..1/4/69

Held Over
By Popular
Demand
★★★★
THE MARVELS
★★★
LITTLE BEAVER
★★★
THE CONTINENTAL DANCERS
★★
FRANK WILLIAM'S
Mighty Rocketeers
★★★★★
THURSDAY NIGHT ONLY
MARCH 28
Sam

Coming April 4
Thurs. Night Only
Gary U.S. Bonds
Ben E. King
Jerry Williams

SHOWS 12:30 & 2:30
$1 before 8 p. m.
lla Williams, D. J.

Pop Weekly Pin-up
No. 8. Dee Dee Sharp

MASHED POTATOES
DEE DEE SHARP

That dance that James Brown always breaks into between screams is called the Mashed Potato. Dee Dee Sharp had megahits with "Mashed Potato Time" and "Gravy (For My Mashed Potatoes)," but she couldn't dance and didn't have a clue as to what the dance was about when she recorded those songs. She said so herself. So the Godfather took up Dee Dee's dancing slack and perfected that dance while singing his own smash,"Mashed Potatoes U.S.A."

When I was performing as Little Jerry Williams in the '60s, I used to do a watered down Mashed Potato. The way I moved my arms could be likened to Mike Tyson losing control of his muscles while delivering nonstop combinations to his opponent... at least until he got knocked out by Buster Douglas!

- *3 pounds white potatoes*
- *½ cup butter*
- *⅓ cup heavy cream*

- Peel potatoes, wash with cold water, dice into reasonable size chunks, place in a pot with enough water to cover. Cover pot with the top slightly askew, bring to a rapid boil. Reduce to medium heat and continue to boil, approximately 20 minutes. Drain potatoes in a colander (don't allow to cool). Place in a bowl and mash with potato masher until lumps have disappeared. Add butter and whip with a spoon until potatoes are smooth and butter has melted completely. Pour in cream, whip 2 minutes more and serve.

(Serves 6)

"GIVE ME VINYL...OR GIVE ME DEATH"

by Swamp Dogg

A medical doctor friend of mine recently purchased new stereo equipment in order to enjoy his new hobby which involves a small, but growing(?) record collection. I put a question mark to denote the inevitable disillusionment my friend will experience when he's made aware of the current vinyl configuration deletion. I didn't have the heart to break it to him as I stood there in his Cleveland home witnessing the system's NASA-like installation by two specialists. The seller flew in from Los Angeles at no(?) cost to my friend. We're talking big bucks here...we're back on the higher-than-giraffe-pussy level. We're talking the following:

Goldman Reference Turntable	$ 30,000
M-300 Audio Research Electronic Power Amps (300 watts)	$ 22,000
SP-15 Pre-amp	$ 6,000
IRS Infinity Speake	$ 50,000
Total	$108,000

Sure, the platter alone weighs 45 pounds (which should interest all of you who lift your platters frequently). It also boasts a computer control tone arm which is about as valuable as a half-pound of afterbirth. And in addition to all of the sweethearts, it has zero tolerance. (So does my wife, and it didn't cost me one hundred and eight thousand dollars to find out.)

I would bet my life that if you combined the playback equipment found in the homes of company heads David Geffen (Geffen Records), Dick Griffey (Solar Records), Mo Ostin (Warner Records), Ahmet Ertegun (Atlantic Records), Bernie Grundman (Bernie Grundman Mastering Lab) and Quincy Jones (Q-West), it would not equal the conglomeration my friend bought, and I'm basing this on the fact that the above people know exactly how much is put into a recording and how much to expect regardless of the playback system. In spite of this, my friend ought to be able to buy vinyl on all catalogs that tout cassettes and compact discs. On the one hand, I think my friend's purchase was ludicrous and on the same hand, he feels that a person has to be shy a little gray matter to purchase a Rolls Royce...in other words, we all do what we want to do after working harder than ten motherfuckers to provide a way.

Vinyl has become the "come in" tool for a "bait and switch" being employed mostly by the industry giants. It's available until the record shows signs of being a massive hit, then it's dropped while still climbing the charts. Now, the retail outlets are embarrassed when they have to tell their customers "no more vinyl, just cassettes and CDs." It's also regrettable that some small independents are getting smaller and less independent, attempting to walk in the major's footsteps. These dumb motherfuckers are discontinuing vinyl, and only making CDs of their popular artists, leaving them ultimately with only cassettes. All of you stupid-ass independents had better wake up and sell more records before you fucking starve to death. The majors can play this game because although they've discontinued vinyl, they didn't delete their network television stations, network radio stations, book divisions, computer game manufacturing, parking lots, motion picture holdings, soft drink stock and so forth.

It is documented by Electric Institute, Washington, D.C., that at the close of 1989 there were 85 million record playback systems and 11.9 million CD players in use throughout America's 91.4 million households. That's 92% with turntables and 14% with CDs. In addition to this, 108,000 turntables were imported in 1987, and although figures aren't available for '88 and '89, you can rest safely with the knowledge that the import figure didn't diminish. Are you going to trash your turntable? I'm definitely not going to trash mine, even though it cost me under a thousand dollars six years back. And I know my buddy in Cleveland is not going to trash his, although he is going to be freaking for the majority of his stereo component life following each visit to a Sound Outhouse or any of its record retail competitors.

Do you remember when the airlines decided to cut back on in-cabin services by discontinuing in-flight movies, using the explanation that they conducted a massive survey which revealed that passengers would rather have some of those sorry ass audio programs in lieu of the first run cinemas? Were you surveyed? Neither was I, or anybody you or I know! So after some real disgruntled passengers threatened them and verbally kicked their asses, they reinstituted the movies with a slight surcharge (all they wanted in the first place)–a way to get a $2.00 rental fee for the headsets. Having this, they could give a monkey fuck.

Or when Detroit announced that people no longer wanted convertibles? Until that time, 1973, a convertible was sold as midline among the particular auto models. A few years later, when the public was groveling, General Motors and their competitors announced that America had not only changed its mind but was willing to pay up the ass for the convertible configuration. They brought them back...shorter, uglier, smaller and definitely more expensive...and they were right; we bought them, and will continue to buy them, as long as they are made available.

The record industry is talking about skyrocketing oil prices; people being more mobile, therefore they aren't listening to music at home; the cow jumped over the moon; Peter Piper can't find his pecker, and any other inanities they can come up with, hoping that the public will say, "Okay! okay! We're willing to pay more for vinyl! We gave Detroit theirs and we're sorry you had to wait so long for yours...we're gapping em', drive it on home."

Did you know that telemarketers are still selling large volumes of 8-track tapes, especially in the country and gospel categories? People will buy what's available, simple as that. Consumers stopped buying argyle socks only because they were no longer being manufactured. Now they are back and consumers are buying them. No, I'm not saying that we actually value those faulty, undependable 8-tracks or those hideous argyle socks. But with eighty-five million turntables in existence, I know that vinyl is not ready to die, and should be re-evaluated by the demigods who are responsible for the murder of vinyl. MI

VEGETABLES
VEGETABLES
VEGETABLES
VEGETABLES
VEGETABLES
VEGETABLES
VEGETABLES
VEGETABLES
VEGETABLES

GENE PITNEY HEARTBREAKER CABBAGE

In the '60s through the early part of '73, they didn't come any better than Gene Pitney. He was writing award-winning songs and going gold all over the world.

I became a Pitney fan in 1961 upon hearing his smashes "(I Wanna) Love My Life Away" and "Every Little Breath I Take." I was hooked from that time to right now. I never had any hopes of meeting this vocal genius, even when I was hired as a staff writer and producer at Musicor, his label.

Gene was visiting Musicor one day and heard me playing and singing down the hall in my little cubicle. He walked down and introduced himself which put me in a real weird position because I'd been instructed by Art Talmadge, Musicor's owner/president, not to have any conversation with Pitney whatsoever. Now here I am meeting a hero and afraid of losing my job for doing so. Well... what the fuck, let's roll with it.

Gene told me that he liked the way I sang and he wanted to make new records with my sound and phrasing. Art Talmadge pretended to be pleased but was royally pissed off at me. Why? Did I drag Gene down the hall? I didn't even know he was in town or in the building. Gene listened to my recording of "Run Run Roadrunner," my effort on Musicor at that time, and said he wanted to record it immediately over the same backing track. So shall it be written, so shall it be done.

The next night we were in Groove Sound (Musicor's studio) taking care of business. Gene liked to listen to my vocal track and sing along to capture my inflections. I was honored then and I'm still honored at this moment. Art was anything but happy with a novice spear-chucker producing his money-generating baby and one of the world's top-ten best, but he bit his tongue because Gene was ecstatic over his new production relationship. Charlie Foxx and I wrote several songs for Pitney including his last smash, "She's a Heartbreaker." If you listen to the vocal track intensely you'll hear me singing under Gene on that song and "Roadrunner" too.

Art Talmadge released "She's a Heartbreaker" under the initials P.G., because he thought I had tainted Gene's image. That didn't stop all of the jocks from recognizing Gene's voice and announcing that it was him. Sales went through the roof, which forced Art to restore Pitney's full name to the record. It went gold-plus, but Art fired me for being disobedient and never paid me a dime, a nickel, a penny, until one afternoon in 1995 when he sent me a check, after being threatened by my attorney, for $84.31. Naturally we sent it back... $84.31 for writing and producing a million-plus selling record? Art's crazier than I look.

Thanks Gene, you're the cream of the crop.

- *1 cabbage (approx. 2½-3 lbs.)*
- *1 medium onion*
- *¼ tsp. crushed red pepper*
- *¼ tsp. garlic powder*
- *5 tbsp. bacon fat*

- Cut cabbage in strips and wash in cold water. Place in colander for about 10 minutes to drain. Put cabbage in Dutch oven without water (cabbage will make its own liquid), and cook over a medium flame in covered pan for 20 minutes. Stir in bacon drippings, diced onion, and garlic powder. Reduce heat and cook in covered pot for 10 minutes. Stir cabbage and replace cover and cook for 20 minutes more.

(Serves 4-6)

Billboard Top 20 Spotlight—Gene Pitney's "She's a Heartbreaker" (Prod. Charlie Foxx) (Writers: Foxx-Williams) (Catalogue/Cee & Eye, BMI)—New blues bag for the stylist and he moves and grooves all the way through this potent Charlie Foxx rocker in top form. Will hit hard and fast and prove one of Pitney's all-time hot sellers. (Catalogue/Primary, BMI). Musicor 1306.

5/4/68

Record Reviews

2/8/69

Picks of the Week

GENE PITNEY (Musicor 1348)
Baby, You're My Kind of Woman (2:50) (Catalogue/Cee & Eye, BMI — Wilbliams, Foxx)

Gene Pitney jumps back into his "Heartbreaker" style for this new blockbuster. Side features his scorching blues-rock vocal powerized by a tremendous beat arrangement. Standout material and Pitney's singular performance give this new venture an immediate impact that should have him back into the breakout lists. Flip: "Hate" (2:59) (Same pubs, BMI — Williams, Harrison, Coley, Foxx)

Reco

Picks of the Week

GENE PITNEY (Musicor 1306)
She's a Heartbreaker (2:59) [Catalogue, Cee & I, BMI—Foxx, Williams]

Smother the vibrant Gene Pitney vocal sound in soul, add a potent rhythmic backing and work up a hefty production; that's the picture with this new effort showing the songster as he has never appeared before. Solid sock and a big combination of vocal and material fires should make an explosive showing on both pop and blues charts. Crashing comeback entry. Flip: "Conquistador" (2:35) [Catalogue, Primary, BMI—Anisfield]

From my first remembrances, I called her Kini, phonetically key-ni. She was Queen Esther Coston, my Aunt Queen, but she remained Kini for me throughout her beautiful life. Libby was her daughter and together they carried me down the roads after they smoothed out the bumps.

Kini is the reason I don't have to wear suspenders today unless I choose to. "Let him wear a goddamn belt if he wants to... like Raymond, Julian, and the other boys... ain't gonna be no sissies round here."

There was nothing on earth too good for me... and nobody on earth good enough for me until I met Yvonne.

Until her death the Leo was the conductor of my life, her life, and the lives of all my aunts, uncles, grandparents, mothers, husbands, pets, and whoever else showed up at her house at 843 Duke Street, Portsmouth, Virginia. She told everyone where to get off, get on and the amount of time they were to maintain a particular situation.

All marriages, and there were many, were performed in Kini's home. All problems were solved in Kini's home.

Kini gave me courage..the funds..to venture further than Portsmouth, to seek success as a singer and songwriter. "Go to New York... get on the Arthur Godfrey show, the Ed Sullivan show. You're better than anyone they've ever had... you're actually too good for 'em."

Well... so much for Kini at this time, but one day soon I'm going to write a book about this great lady and share a fantastic person with all.

To her I was always her junior and I've never wanted to be something so much again in all my life.

I love you Kini.

DOO WOP SQUASH

We had squash on our plates at least once a week when I was growing up around my Aunt Kini. She would rent rooms in our house for musicians that would come into Portsmouth, during the doo-wop era. We only had two hotels in town. But they were white; niggers couldn't go in. So people stayed with Kini.

I remember one time, Fats Domino and a bunch of other people came through after a law passed saying blacks could stay in the same hotels as whites, on the same floors and stuff. Fats stayed at The Americana Hotel in Portsmouth, as it was called at that time But the hotel's owners weren't ready for all this. Fats and everyone jumped in the pool with their head rags on and everything. "Fuck y'all," they said. "Y'all not going to swim with our water." They drained the pool while they were in it. Staying at the Americana wasn't like staying at Aunt Kini's.

You can eat a bowl of squash and not have anything else. Because you always put something in it like a sausage, and you cut up some sausage, a little ham. You need a little pork in it. Beef ain't going to do it. But squash, it's delicious-just like Kini made it.

- *6 medium-size squashes about 1½ pounds total*
- *4 tablespoons bacon fat*
- *1 onion*
- *½ tablespoon pepper*
- *¼ teaspoon salt*
- *3 italian hot sausages*
- *⅔ cup water*

- Wash squash good with a vegetable brush. Heat bacon fat in fry pan, cut squash into ¼ inch pieces. Dice onion. Add squash and onion to bacon fat, cover, and cook over a medium flame. Cook for 10 minutes. Add salt and pepper. Stir and cook 10 minutes stirring frequently. Add Italian hots and continue to cook for 15 minutes. Cut each sausage into sections of four and continue to cook for 20 minutes more. Add ⅓ cup of water and cook another 10 minutes.

- Serve with rice or as is.

(Serves 8)

"IF I CAN"T BE YOUR HUSBAND, LET ME BE YOUR WIFE"

by Swamp Dogg

I've written this article several times in the last few days, attempting to ward off some of the controversy that my writing has been generating. I've been accused of being too black... Take a look at my picture, I'm lighter than Idi Amin, which is some black for your ass in more ways than one. I've been verbally chastised for the use of profanity...To those whom I've offended I say fuck you!

I started to write about the un-even-ness of the pollings/surveys that our industry's Koran, *Billboard*, does each week in tracking stores to determine the records to bump and the records to dump. In preparation for this, I enlisted two watts lines and tracked over three hundred stores in Chicago, Los Angeles, and the areas which they influence, that sell predominantly country and black, and are not located in malls and are independently owned. We asked them the following questions:

(1) Are you a *Billboard* reporter?
(2) If so, how often do they call you?
(3) Are you independently owned?

Of the three hundred retailers, twenty-five were reporters. Most stores don't have a clue how a record gets on the charts. This means only one thing: if your record is not in a mall store—which is usually a chain—you will not be accounted for, because the *Billboard* survey is directed largely towards mall stores and Mount Rushmore-type chains; which, by the way, was a controversial issue when Tone Loc's "Wild Thing" single climbed to #2 on the pop singles chart and was outselling everything in the top five, and *Billboard* sent a message to the effect that several mall stores had not even felt this excitement; therefore to dream of #1, was synonymous with pissing in the wind. With this in mind, I decided to leave this subject alone because I did not want to piss off Bill, the chairman of the Board.

My next idea was to write an article on the new record airplay measuring method called Broadcast Data Systems (BDS). This system is set up like a Neilsen and tracks records that are played on BDS-monitored stations on a twenty-four hour, nonstop basis.

The owners of this system, BIP COMMUNICATIONS, say that they will be tracking 725 radio and television stations in the 75 most important markets in the United States. What infallible mind determined these markets? How many radio stations? How many television stations? Does this mean that the old system was less than correct and we were being fed erroneous info? It was announced that country music radio had been elected to be the guinea pig. If it fails, let it fail on country which is the true heritage of the white man in America, not Aerosmith, as some would lead us to believe.

Turning our backs on sales—because we don't happen to relate to what's selling—and instead using airplay to determine popularity, is exactly what raped and murdered radio during the disco era. Refusing to accept that disco was selling, and would continue to sell based on the belief that "it's just for gays," put the majors in the shit house. We must acknowledge sales, regardless of the source, if we plan to remain a record business. That's one of the rudiments of economics.

After learning that BPI COMMUNICATIONS was the publisher of *Billboard* I decided not to write about this subject—mainly because I felt that *Billboard* did not need me to tell them that if they continued to employ these methods, they would become an industry joke. Bigger gods have tasted the dust.

Well, why not write about how the public is all over the record industry's back to put on warning stickers, execute those who rap dirty lyrics and burn stores that stock Two Live Crew and their exponents who give birth to this so-called filth. Before I continue, please don't throw out Frank Zappa because I love the way he raps:

I whipped off her bloomers 'n stiffened my thumb
And applied rotation on her sugar plum
I poked and stroked till my wrist got numb
But I still didn't hear no Dinah-MOE Humm
Kiss my aura... Dora
M-M-M...it's real angora
Would you like some more-a?
Right there on the flora?

...or my John and Yoko, *Two Virgins* masterpiece which allowed me to explore their entire anatomy... just a fantasy of mine to that date. My point? These specialized productions were not unlike today's crotch grabbers. These records have to be sniffed out of shops by those who will go to all lengths to obtain the works of a handful of daring artists who sometimes take walks down *rue de risque*. We are seeing new rap bluebloods like M.C. Hammer, Fresh Prince, Daddy D, Beatmaster Clay D & Get Fresh Crew, Heavy D and Young M.C., who are not utilizing unnecessarily foul language in their raps, and have some classy material that's selling. Nevertheless, when you lump em' all together, you at least know what they're about before you buy them, unlike our entertainment counterpart, the cinema, which happens to be the real culprit, if there even is one. The movies will take a child of any verbal age and teach him to speak foul language that would shame the most loose-moraled adult. A perfect example of this occurred in Eddie Murphy's *Harlem Nights*, where a small boy portraying Eddie used obscenities galore and murdered a man in cold blood as the *coup de grace*. *Staying Together*, starring Sean Austin, touted three teenage brothers who lived for sex with older women and had mastered the art of profanity... *Stand By Me*, with River Phoenix, highlighted blue language throughout. I am neither condemning nor exalting these situations...I just want to know what makes River Phoenix right for the children, and Ice T wrong? I decided against this article also... too many questions , too few answers.

Since I can't muster up subject matter that's apropos for my six avid readers, and due to the fact that I don't like to make people angry until at least sixty days after Xmas, I am not writing anything for this issue. MI

ScREECH!
ScREECH!

DESSERTS DESSERTS DESSERTS DESSERTS DESSERTS DESSERTS DESSERTS

#2 WITH A BULLET: APPLE PARTY DESSERT

In music vernacular, a bullet denotes a popular recording that's moving more rapidly than its competition and a track is a synonym, in the recording studio, for a channel. In the studio, each VU meter identifies each separate track. E.g., we'll have guitars on track one, bass on track two, keyboards on track three, etc., etc., up to 124 tracks or more if necessary. I wrote up a few of my more intricate recipes in tracks because it might make them more easy to follow.

TRACK I

- *5 lbs. of green apples*
- *2 tbsp. nutmeg*
- *1 tbsp. cinnamon*
- *5 tbsp. of sugar*
- *3½ cups all-purpose flour sifted*
- *⅓ cup sugar*
- *1 cup vegetable shortening*
- *⅔ cup ice water*

- Peel and slice apples, put in a large baking dish, sprinkle 4 cups of sugar, cinnamon, and nutmeg over apples and add 4 tbsp. of water. Let stand for 1 hour. Remove apple mixture and place in a large pot with remaining sugar and 3 cups of water and place over a low flame, cook for 1 hour.

- Sift flour and sugar into mixing bowl. Add shortening. Cut in with a pastry blender or two knives until mixture looks like peas. Sprinkle the water over the flour a tbsp. at a time, stirring the mixture with a fork until enough water has been added to form the dough into a ball. Wrap the dough in wax paper and chill for ½ hour. Roll out ½ the dough on a floured board and line the sides and bottom of a large baking pan with dough.

TRACK II

- *1½ cups flour*
- *2 tsp. baking powder*
- *1½ cups sugar*
- *2 beaten eggs*
- *1⅓ cup milk*
- *8 oz. melted butter*
- *1 tsp. vanilla*

- Sift together flour, baking powder, and sugar in a bowl, then add eggs and milk, etc. Add this mixture to the apples, mix well, and then pour apples and batter into the pan lined with dough. Roll out the remaining dough and cut into 1-inch strips and lay crisscross over the top of the baking dish. Leave at least 2- to 3-inch opening "that the apples may peep through." Place in a 400-degree oven for 20 minutes. Reduce to 350 degrees and continue to bake for 1 hour.

- Remove from oven. Separate 1 egg and beat egg yolk, spread egg yolk over the top of the dough lightly with a pastry brush. Put back in 350-degree oven for 10 minutes or until brown on top.

(Serves 10-12)

Debbie... my oldest daughter... she eats it all and doesn't gain a pound... 80'

Cliff Shaw a/k/a Karimu. Always dieting but he puts it back at my house...

J.D. Bryant, Denise Dail, and Dave "Baby" Cortez headed to Muscle Shoals to record. Charlie Whitehead's "Love Being Your Fool" hit came out of this wild ass session. Remind me to tell you about it.

Chris Blackwell in my kitchen... loving the aroma ('75)

Chris Blackwell didn't know a nigger could make cheesecake

BUSTER BROWN CHEESE CAKE

You know that song about Buster Brown? "I live in a shoe, this is my dog Tag, he lives in here too"... and a funky, unsanitary home it was. Wrong Buster Brown. This recipe is for the harmonica-playing, blues-singing, pot-bellied, cheesecake-eating motherfucker from Criss County, Georgia, who recorded several hit records including "Fannie Mae" and "Is You Is or Is You Ain't My Baby," which achieved gold record status on Bobby Robinson's Fire label. Who's Bobby Robinson? An R'n'B pioneer who was responsible for the first hit records by Gladys Knight and the Pips, Wilbert Harrison, Jerry Butler, and Don Covay, plus Kurtis Blow, Melle Mel, and several hundred more... But Buster Brown was one of his greats.

TRACK I (CRUST)

- *1 springform pan (9 inch)**
- *1 cup flour (sifted 3 times)*
- *¼ cup sugar*
- *1 tsp. grated lemon peel*
- *½ cup butter*
- *2 egg yolks (beaten)*
- *½ tsp. vanilla*

- Mix flour, sugar, and lemon peel together. Using a pastry blender, cut butter and flour mixture until it resembles coarse crumbs. Mix in egg yolks and vanilla, then pat ⅓ of the crust on the bottom of the springform pan. Remove the sides and bake bottom at 400 degrees for 10 minutes. Let bottom cool, then attach the sides. Butter the sides and pat remaining crust on the sides.

TRACK II (CAKE)

- *5 8oz. packages cream cheese*
- *¼ tsp. vanilla*
- *1 tsp. grated lemon peel*
- *1¾ cups sugar*
  3 tbsp. flour
- *6 eggs*
- *2 egg whites*
- *¼ cup whipping cream*

- Put cheese in a large mixing bowl and let it sit at room temperature for 3 hours. Then beat it until partially smooth. Add vanilla and lemon peel and continue to beat. Mix sugar and flour together, then add slowly to cheese, beating constantly until smooth. Add the eggs and egg whites one at a time, beating constantly. After the last egg has been added, beat for 10 minutes more. Whip the cream until semi-stiff, then gently fold into the batter. Turn the mixture into a springform pan and bake for 10 minutes at 450 degrees. Then reduce the oven to 300 degrees for 1 hour or until you can insert a knife and extract it clean of cake mixture.

- Let cool for 30 minutes, then loosen the sides of the pan. Cool 30 minutes more, then gently take the sides off. Let the cake stand another 1½ hours, then place in refrigerator.

- A can of cherry or blueberry pie filling is good chilled and served on top of each slice.

(Serves 12-16)

ROCK UPSIDE DOWN FRUIT CAKE ROLL

Delete "Upside Down Fruit Cake" and you're left with the love of my life, rock 'n' roll.

- *¼ cup butter*
- *1 cup brown sugar*
- *1 cup pecan nutmeats*
- *1 30oz. can fruit cocktail*
- *1 tbsp. lemon juice*
- *Cottage Pudding Batter (see below)**

- Preheat oven to 400 degrees.

- Melt butter in a heavy frying pan. Spread brown sugar evenly over the melted butter. Sprinkle the nutmeats over the butter sugar mixture. Drain all of the juice off the fruit cocktail and spread over the nutmeats. Sprinkle the lemon juice evenly over the fruit cocktail. Cover with the Cottage Pudding.*

- Bake 40 minutes or until the top is brown and crusty. Turn out on a serving dish immediately, fruit side up, or it will stick.

COTTAGE PUDDING*

- *1½ cups all-purpose flour*
- *2 tbsp. baking powder*
- *½ cup of sugar*
- *1 egg*
- *½ cup milk*
- *½ cup melted butter*

- Sift flour, baking powder, and sugar together. Mix well-beaten egg, milk, and melted butter together. Stir gently into flour mixture.

(Serves 8)

Red Hot Nutz
Roasted Peanuts
THE WINE SHOP
Red Hot Nutz
Roasted Peanuts
Chocolate Covered Nutz

Cousin Libby and her husband Luther. Libby was too great to be just a cousin; she was always an aunt to me. She was there for my first everything.... day of school, doctor's visit, school play, piano recital, whatever. She loved me and I loved her in return. She started teaching me to cook when I was about four or five years old. Thank you, Libby, for everything. I love you.

LIBBY'S PORTSMOUTH PEACH COBBLER

Libby Lorenzo Lanier, my dear aunt, taught me at an early age the virtues of folding batter as opposed to cutting in butter, as opposed to cutting school or beating eggs, as opposed to beating my friends or heating oil as opposed to heated arguments.

I'll always love her.

- *1 stick (½ cup) butter*
- *1 cup flour*
- *1 cup sugar*
- *1 tbsp. baking powder*
- *1 tsp. vanilla*
- *1 cup milk*
- *½ tbsp. rum flavoring*
- *½ tsp. nutmeg*
- *1 29oz. can sliced sweetened peaches (retain some juice)*

- In a 350-degree oven melt butter in a 6½-by-12-inch baking dish. Combine flour, sugar, baking powder, nutmeg, vanilla, and milk. Stir until well blended. Pour batter over melted butter. Drain juice off of peaches, then top the batter with the peaches and stir around evenly until peaches are distributed throughout the batter. Bake in 350-degree oven for about 1 hour or until top crust is golden brown.

- This recipe that has been handed down through my family for approximately one hundred and seventy-five years. Through you I intend to preserve it in kitchens throughout the world till the end of time... then some. If you would like to do it the way my great, great, great, greats did it... use fresh peaches that have been soaked in sugar approximately 8 hours in the refrigerator. My personal serving suggestion is to top each serving with vanilla ice cream or lemon sauce.

(Serves 10)

LIBBY'S GRATED SWEET POTATO PUDDING

My Aunt Libby was more like a parent. She couldn't have children so she bestowed all of that love on me, and as I look back to my childhood, I needed it.

1971 found me very successful and I went home to see my parents driving a new Rolls Royce accompanied by my bodyguards who were driving my two new Lincoln Continentals. Yes, I was showing off and I needed bodyguards about as much as a bull needed tits... I digress. After several days of visiting, we prepared to go back to New York. As I was walking out the door, Libby walked up to me, gave me a big hug and kiss, then slipped a twenty-dollar bill into my hand with a "take it baby, anything can happen out there." That was love. She had seen a million motherfuckers come through town acting like Donald Trump worked for them and didn't have funds to get through the Midtown tunnel. I took it and sent it back in presents quadrupled.

- *2 large uncooked sweet potatoes*
- *1½ cups sugar (more if the season has not produced a good crop of sweet potatoes)*
- *1 tbsp. vanilla*
- *2 cans of evaporated milk*
- *3 eggs beaten*
- *2 tbsp. all-purpose flour*
- *2 sticks of butter*

- Preheat oven to 400 degrees.

- Peel and finely grate the raw sweet potatoes. Melt butter and add to potatoes. Add beaten eggs, vanilla, milk, sugar, and flour to potato mixture. Stir until well blended. Bake in a large baking dish for 55 minutes.

- Serve hot or cold as a dessert.

(Serves 10)

Moogstar

Jesus just knocked on your door

Whose got the nerve to let Him in?

Z.Z.HILL

"A MAN NEEDS A WOMAN"

MANKIND 12017

A Jerry Williams Production

FROM THE ALBUM "THE BRAND NEW Z.Z. HILL"

Mankind 201, 8 Track 80201

Distributed By Nasl

Z.Z. HILL FRIED APPLES

Z.Z. Hill was a late bloomer musically, who made critically acclaimed blues records in the '60s for Kent Records and reached his first hit peak with "Don't Make Me Pay For His Mistakes" on a label jointly owned by his brother Matt Hill, Miles Grayson, and himself. I met Z.Z. after he signed to my Mankind record label but didn't know it. How'd it happen? He was originally signed to Phil Walden's Capricorn label, but because of irreconcilable differences, Phil sold the contract to Percy Sledge's producer and the owner of Quinvy records, Quinn Ivy, who Z.Z. also had problems with.

I was in Muscle Shoals, Alabama, without any knowledge of the irreconcilables, when Quinn offered to sell me Z.Z.'s contract and recorded masters. I jumped right in bed with Quinn only to discover that Z.Z. does not want to deal with me because I'm a good friend of Quinn and Phil and he just knows that I'm going to be worse than the both of them rolled into one. After about two months of pursuing him to explain my position and introduce myself, we finally checked into the same hotel in New Orleans and conversed. I could not change his mind about me. Some people had convinced Z.Z. that if he'd signed with United Artists he would go pop like Anka, Sinatra, Mathis... I couldn't convince him otherwise. But I agreed to give him a release of contract if he would allow me to produce one album for him. We met at Quinvy studio in Muscle Shoals. He learned the songs, we recorded, got to know each other a little better. He left, I left.

From this session came the legendary *Blues at the Opera* LP. It spawned five hit singles including "The Chokin' Kind," "Faithful and True," and "Second Chance." Within a year, Z.Z. and I had become good friends. I booked some concerts with him and had the distinct pleasure of being a part of his leap to fame in 1981 by writing the B side to the "Cheating In The Next Room" single, "Right Arm For Your Love." "Right Arm" was strong but when the disc jockeys and the public, including myself, heard "Cheating," it was no contest as to what the A side should have been... so it was flipped over and Z.Z. became a blues superstar to rival B.B. King. Bobby Bland was his opening act.

I hate this part... Z.Z. died. He wasn't old. Something about a blood clot that formed when he broke his leg.

Some of the best blues records ever cut were cut by Z.Z. Hill, a good man.

- *1 lb. apples (cored and sliced thick)*
- *¼ cup butter*
- *1 tbsp. bacon drippings*
- *1 tsp. nutmeg*
- *¼ cup brown sugar*
- *⅓ cup sugar*

- In a fry pan heat bacon drippings and add butter. Put apples in pan and sprinkle with nutmeg and both kinds of sugar. Stir fry constantly over a high flame until brown and crisp.

- Remove from pan and serve immediately or they will become mushy.

(Serves 4)

YVONNE'S TOMATO PUDDING 33⅓ RPM

My wife, manager, lover, buddy, and confidant, Yvonne, loved this dish and would kill for it. There were times when I'd make it twice in one week for her and she still remained slender, tender and tall. Libby taught me this one also but she learned it from my Aunt Kini, her mother.

This fantastic dish has to be done in two steps, but the end results will make every step worth its weight in calories.

TRACK I (8 CRUSTY BISCUITS)

- *2 cups all-purpose flour*
- *2 tbsp. vegetable shortening*
- *⅔ cup cold water (do not substitute milk)*
- *1 tsp. baking powder*

- Preheat oven to 450 degrees.

- Combine flour, baking powder, and shortening. Mix together thoroughly with spoon or hands. Pour in water gradually while working pastry together. When flour is soft and light, not sticky, turn out on floured board. With floured hands pat dough until smooth. Roll into an oblong and cut out 8 biscuits. Place on ungreased baking sheet 1 inch apart and bake for 15 minutes.

- No, do not use canned biscuits under any circumstances.

TRACK II (PUDDING)

- *1 16 oz. can peeled tomatoes*
- *1 cup sugar*
- *8 oz. butter (melted)*
- *1 tsp. nutmeg*
- *8 large biscuits*

- Put tomatoes in a bowl and mash with a potato masher. Add butter, sugar, and nutmeg, stir until blended. After the biscuits have baked remove from oven and reduce heat to 400 degrees. Wait 5 minutes and put tomato mixture in the oven for 30 minutes, in a 2-quart baking dish. Remove the tomato mixture from the oven and add biscuits crumbled up in tomato mixture. Stir and place in oven and bake until biscuits are golden brown.

- This is another great dessert to serve at those times when you are bored with the norm.

(Serves 6)

Congratulations
Jerry + Yvonne
July 7, 2001

Recorded by LITTLE JERRY WILLIAMS on Loma Records

I'M THE LOVER MAN

Words and Music by JERRY WILLIAMS

DISCOGRAPHY

THERE AIN'T ENOUGH LOVE
LITTLE JERRY
1961, Ember Records

(I'LL ALWAYS REMEMBER) CHAPEL ON THE HILL
LITTLE JERRY
1962, Aldo Records

LET'S DO THE WOBBLE
JERRY WILLIAMS
1962, V-Tone Records

I'M THE LOVER MAN / THE PUSH PUSH PUSH
LITTLE JERRY WILLIAMS
1964, Southern Sound Records

BABY, YOU'RE MY EVERYTHING
LITTLE JERRY WILLIAMS
1965, Calla Records

BABY BUNNY (SUGAR HONEY)
JERRY WILLIAMS
1965, Calla Records

DETROIT/THE 1965 KING SIZE NICOTINE BLUES
LITTLE JERRY WILLIAMS
1965, Southern Sound Records

HUM-BABY / SHE'S SO DIVINE
LITTLE JERRY WILLIAMS
1965, Academy Records

IF YOU ASK ME (BECAUSE I LOVE YOU) / YVONNE
JERRY WILLIAMS
1966, Calla Records

WHAT'S THE MATTER WITH YOU BABY
JERRY WILLIAMS
1967, Calla Records

YOUR MAN / GIVE THE DISC JOCKEY SOME
JERRY WILLIAMS
1967, 87-30 Records

RUN RUN ROADRUNNER / I'M IN THE DANGER ZONE
JERRY WILLIAMS
1967, Musicor Records

I GOT WHAT IT TAKES
BROOKS & JERRY
1968, Cotillion Records

SHIPWRECKED
JERRY WILLIAMS
1969, Cotillion Records

COME AND GET IT / IT'S STILL GOOD
JERRY WILLIAMS
1969, Cotillion Records

WHEN YOU MOVE, YOU LOSE / THAT'S THE GROOVE
JERRY WILLIAMS
2004, Grapevine Records

OH LORD, WHAT ARE YOU DOING TO ME /
IF YOU'RE LEAVING (TAKE ME WITH YOU)
JERRY WILLIAMS / SWAMP DOGG, 2020, Soul 4 Real Records

18 **IF YOU ASK ME (BECAUSE I LOVE YOU) / WHAT SHALL I DO**
JERRY WILLIAMS / FRANKIE & THE CLASSICALS
2023, Stateside Records

19 **MAMA'S BABY, DADDY'S MAYBE**
SWAMP DOGG
1970, Salafaster

20 **SYNTHETIC WORLD / TOTAL DESTRUCTION TO YOUR MIND**
SWAMP DOGG
1970, Salafaster

21 **THESE ARE NOT MY PEOPLE / I WAS BORN BLUE**
SWAMP DOGG
1971, Salafaster

22 **CREEPING AWAY / DO YOU BELIEVE**
SWAMP DOGG
1972, Elektra Records

23 **SAM STONE / KNOWING I'M PLEASING ME AND YOU**
SWAMP DOGG
1973, Cream Records

24 **BUZZARD LUCK / EBONY AND JET**
SWAMP DOGG
1973, Brut Records

25 **STRAIGHT FROM MY HEART / DON'T THROW YOU LOVE TO THE WIND**
SWAMP DOGG
1973, Swamp Dogg Presents Records

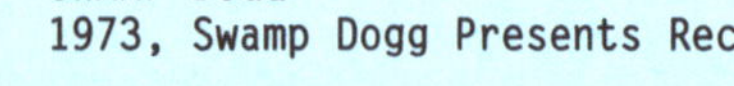

26 **WIFESITTER / PLEASE LET ME KISS YOU GOODBYE**
SWAMP DOGG
1973, Stone Dogg Records

27 **MIGHTY MIGHTY DOLLAR BILL /**
CHOKING TO DEATH (FROM THE TIES THAT BIND)
SWAMP DOGG, 1973, Stone Dogg Records

28 **I WANNA LIFETIME OF LOVING YOU /**
DID I COME BACK TOO SOON OR DID I STAY AWAY TOO LONG
SWAMP DOGG, 1974, Island Records

29 **THE OTHER MAN / BELIEVE IN ME BABY**
SWAMP DOGG
1976, DJM Records

30 **I SURE LOVE TO BALL / I DID IT ALL**
SWAMP DOGG
1977, Wizard Records

31 **MY HEART JUST CAN'T STOP / DANCING / SILLY SILLY SILLY ME**
SWAMP DOGG
1977, Musicor Records

32 **COME ON AND DANCE WITH ME / SALTY DOG**
SWAMP DOGG
1979, Atomic Art Records

33 **RIGHT ARM FOR YOUR LOVE / COME GET IT**
SWAMP DOGG
1982, ALA Records

34 **THIS IS IT / ALL SHE WANTS IS REGGAE MUSIC**
SWAMP DOGG
1983, Rare Bullet Records

35 **SHUT YOUR MOUTH / MOUTH MUSIC**
SWAMP DOGG
1985, Rare Bullet Records

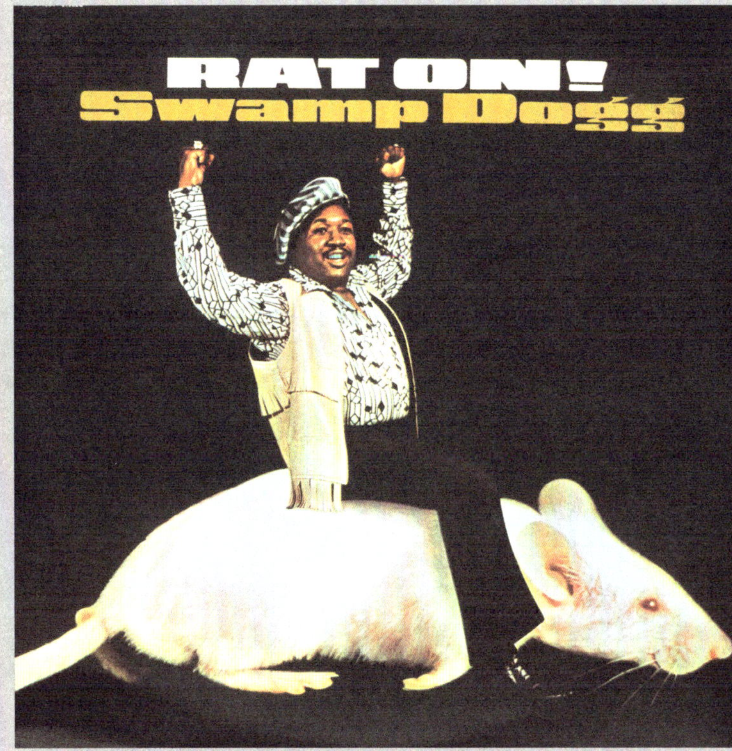

1

TOTAL DESTRUCTION TO YOUR MIND
SWAMP DOGG
1970, Canyon Records.

2

RAT ON!
SWAMP DOGG
1971, Elektra Records.

3

CUFFED, COLLARED AND TAGGED
SWAMP DOGG
1972, Cream.

4

GAG A MAGGOTT
SWAMP DOGG
1972, Stone Dogg Records.

HAVE YOU HEARD THIS STORY??
SWAMP DOGG
1974, Island Records.

SWAMP DOGG'S GREATEST HITS?
SWAMP DOGG
1976, Stone Dogg Records.

YOU AIN'T NEVER TOO OLD TO BOOGIE
SWAMP DOGG
1976, DJM Records.

FINALLY CAUGHT UP WITH MYSELF
SWAMP DOGG
1977, Musicor Records.

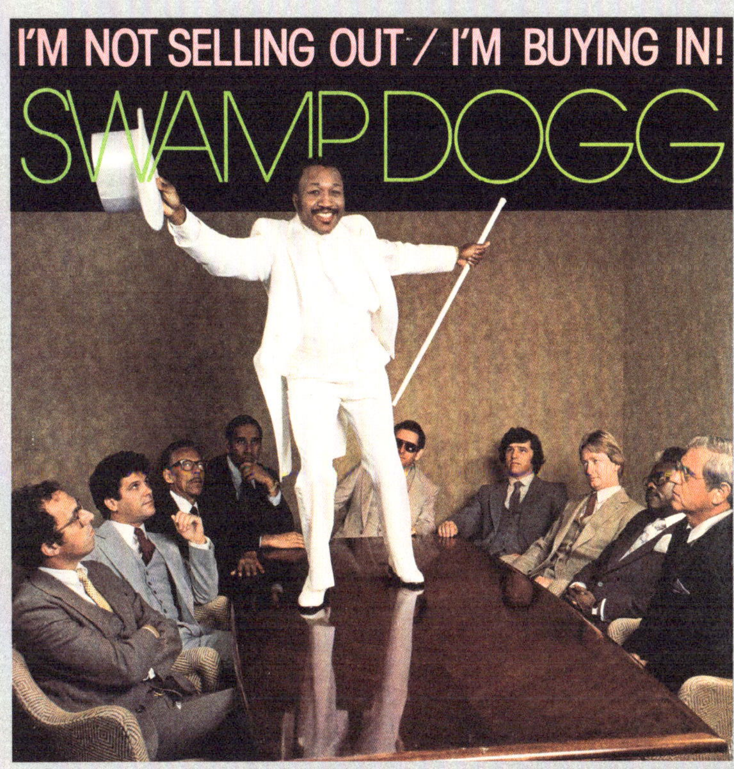

AN OPPORTUNITY... NOT A BARGAIN!!!
SWAMP DOGG
1977, Wizard Records.

I'M NOT SELLING OUT / I'M BUYING IN!
SWAMP DOGG
1981, Tacoma Records

UNCUT AND CLASSIFIED 1A
SWAMP DOGG
1981, Charly Records.

BEST OF SWAMP DOGG... 13 PRIME WEINERS
SWAMP DOGG, 1982, War Bride Records.

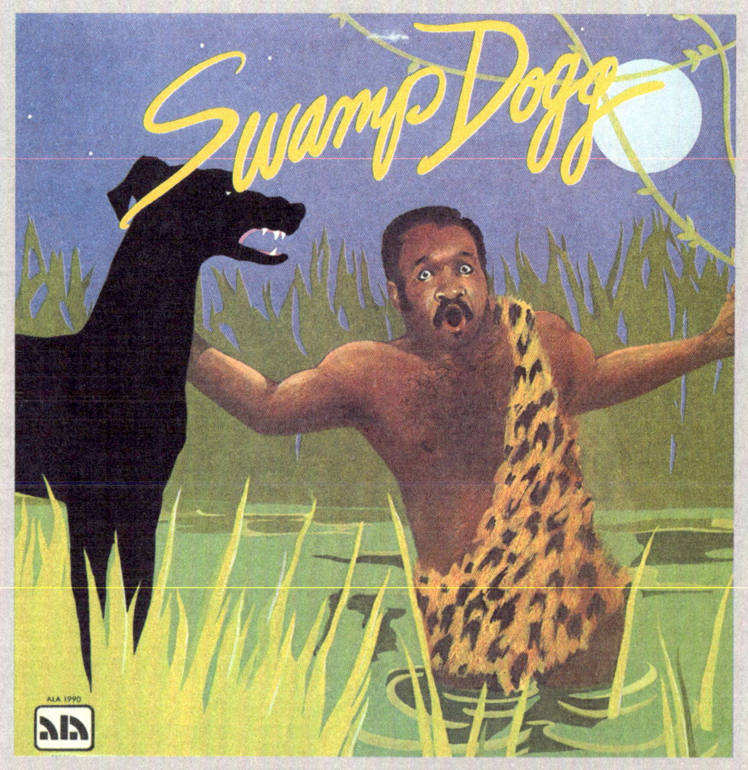

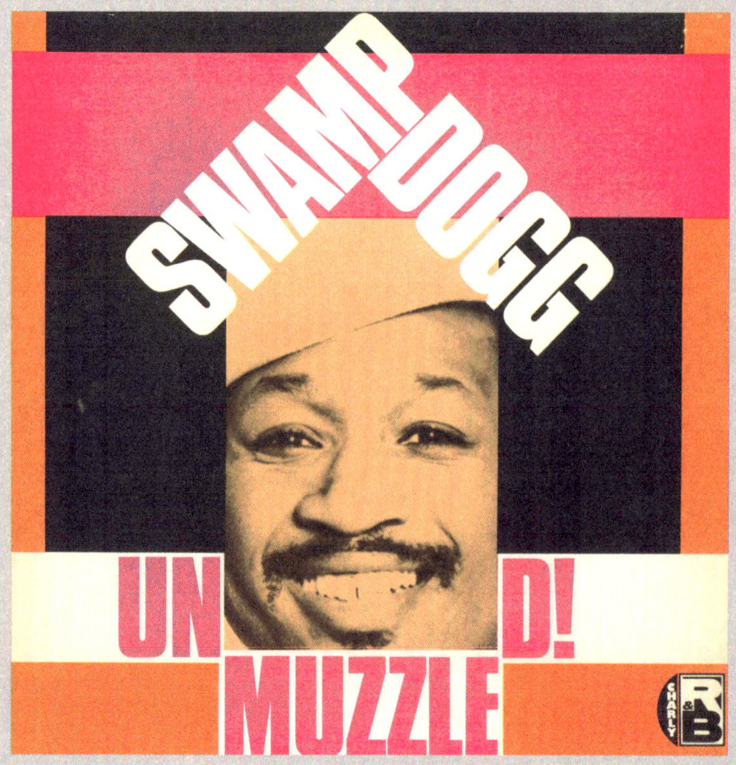

SWAMP DOGG
SWAMP DOGG
1982, ALA Records.

DANCIN' WITH SOUL
SWAMP DOGG
1983, Rare Bullet Records.

UNMUZZLED!
SWAMP DOGG
1983, Charly Records.

I CALLED FOR A ROPE AND THEY THREW ME A ROCK
SWAMP DOGG
1989, S.D.E.G. Records.

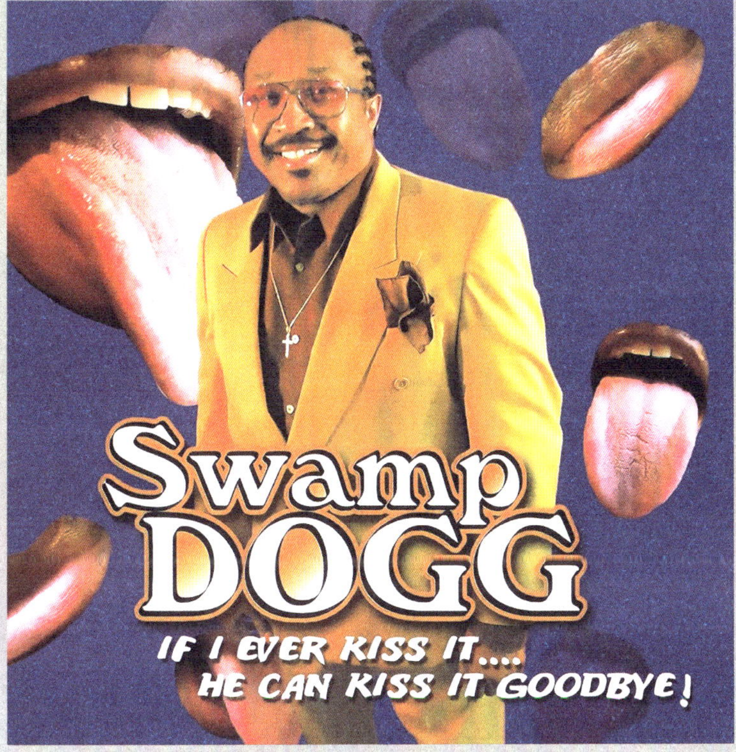

17

SURFIN' IN HARLEM
SWAMP DOGG
1991, Volt Records.

18

THE RE-INVENTION OF SWAMP DOGG
SWAMP DOGG
2000, S.D.E.G. Records.

19

IF I EVER KISS IT.... HE CAN KISS IT GOODBYE!
SWAMP DOGG
2002, S.D.E.G. Records.

20

RESURRECTION
SWAMP DOGG
2007, S.D.E.G. Records.

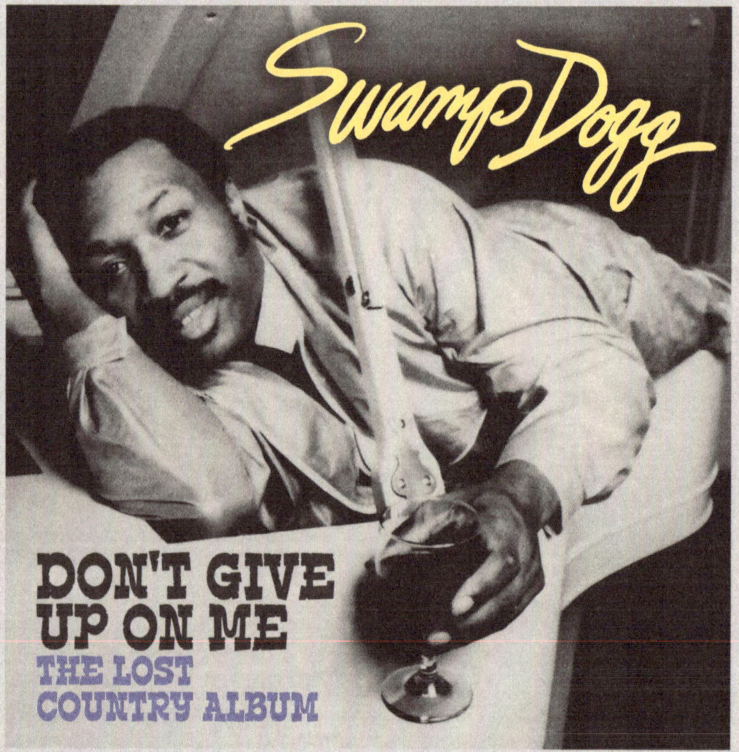

21 **GIVE 'EM AS LITTLE AS YOU CAN... AS OFTEN AS YOU HAVE TO... OR... A TRIBUTE TO ROCK 'N' ROLL**
SWAMP DOGG, 2009, S.D.E.G. Records.

22 **AN AWFUL CHRISTMAS AND A LOUSY NEW YEAR**
SWAMP DOGG
2009 S.D.E.G. Records.

23 **THE WHITE MAN MADE ME DO IT**
SWAMP DOGG
2014, S.D.E.G. Records.

24 **DON'T GIVE UP ON ME: THE LOST COUNTRY ALBUM**
SWAMP DOGG
2013, Essential Media Mod.

25 **LOVE, LOSS, AND AUTO-TUNE**
SWAMP DOGG
2018, Joyful Noise Recordings.

26 **SORRY YOU COULDN'T MAKE IT**
SWAMP DOGG
2020, Pioneer Works Press & Joyful Noise Recordings.

27 **I NEED A JOB... SO I CAN BUY MORE AUTO-TUNE**
SWAMP DOGG
2022, Don Giovanni.

28 **BLACKGRASS: FROM WEST VIRGINIA TO 125TH ST**
SWAMP DOGG
2024, Oh Boy Records.

If You Can Kill It
I Can Cook It
by Swamp Dogg

Published by
Pioneer Works Press

Editors: Gabriel Florenz,
Joshua Jelly-Schapiro
Managing Editor:
Micaela Durand
Art Direction: Daniel Kent
Designers: Daniel Kent,
Callum Abbott
Design Assistance:
Mei Lenehan
Copy Editor: Drew Zeiba
Special Advisors:
Isaac Gale, Ryan Olson

Special thanks to Jeri Y. Williams, Moogstar, Molly Menard, JoLynn Garnes, Jesse Willenbring, Paul Lovelace

Typefaces: CMU Typerwriter Text, Letter Gothic MT, Cooper BT

Distribution
ARTBOOK | D.A.P. USA
75 Broad Street, Suite 630
New York, NY 10004
ArtBook.com

Distribution in EU / UK
Public Knowledge Books
90 Hoe Street,
London, E17 4QS
PublicKnowledgeBooks.com

Printed and bound by
die Keure

First Edition

Pioneer Works Press
159 Pioneer Street
Brooklyn, NY 11231
PioneerWorks.org

ISBN 978-1-945711-21-3

Pioneer Works Press is the publishing imprint of the arts and science organization Pioneer Works, dedicated to supporting experimental and pathbreaking work from leading artists and writers in contemporary culture.

All photos courtesy of Swamp Dogg, with the following exceptions:

P.22 Quincy Jones (Los Angeles Times/Wikimedia Commons/CC-BY 4.0), P.22 Quincy Jones (Eric Koch for Anefo/Wikimedia Commons/CCO 1.0), P.47 T Bone Walker (Harold F. Oxley Agency/ Wikimedia Commons/PD), P.48 BB King (Gorupdebesanez/ Wikimedia Commons/CC BY-SA 3.0, P.48 BB King (Eugene F. Tourangeau/Wikimedia Commons/PDP.51 Hank Williams Jr (MGM Records/ Wikimedia Commons/PD), P.60 Tone Loc (John Atashian/ Alamy), P.68 Temptations (Everett Collection/ Alamy), P.71 Albert Collins (Masahiro Sumori/Wikimedia Commons/CC BY-SA 3.0), P.71 Albert Collins (John Atashian/Alamy), P.83 Jerry Lee Lewis (Bill Waterson/ Alamy/PD), P.84 LL Cool J (John Matthew Smith/ CC BY-SA 2.0), P.84 LL Cool J (EditorialFotos/ Alamy), P.83 Louis Jordan (J. Walter Thompson/ Wikimedia Commons/PD), P.84 Fats Domino (Hugo van Gelderen for Anefo/ Wikimedia Commons/CCO 1.0), P.84 Fats Domino (Hugo van Gelderen for Anefo/Wikimedia Commons/ CCO 1.0), P.103 Guitar Slim (Pictorial Press Ltd/ Alamy), P.115 Fats Waller (Alan Fisher/Library of Congress/PD), P.119 Big Maybelle (Pictorial Press Ltd/Alamy), P.124 Wynonie Harris (Unknown/Wikimedia Commons/PD), P.124 Wynonie Harris (Pictorial Press Ltd/Alamy), P.128 James Brown (Koen Suyk for Anefo/ Wikimedia Commons/CCO 1.0), P.137 Lionel Hampton (William P. Gottlieb/ Library of Congress/ PD), P.138 Sam Cook (Bradford Timeline/Flickr/ CC BY-NC 2.0), P.138 Sam Cook (ca1951rr/Flickr/ CC BY-NC-SA 2.0), P.142 Pigmeat Markham (Vinyls/ Alamy), P.145 Charley Pride (National Archives/ PD), P.149 Willie Nelson (Atlantic Records/Wikimedia Commons/PD, P.150 George Jones (Pictorial Press Ltd/ Alamy, P.153 James Taylor: photo unknown/Wikimedia Commons/PD, P.154 Otis Redding (Bill Waterson/ Alamy, P.162 Dee Dee Sharp (Bradford Timeline/Flickr/ CC BY-NC 2.0)

Swamp Dogg
Swamp Dogg
Dizzy Fae

1-866-DOGG-FUD

My wife, Yvonne at two-and-a-half years old and her half sister Lillian. Without Yvonne by my side to urge me on I'd give less than two fucks about cooking anything. I'd eat out forever and would turn my kitchen into a pool room, brothel, whatever...

I love you Yvonne.